WHAT SHALL WE SAY ABOUT ALCOHOL?

CARADINE R. HOOTON

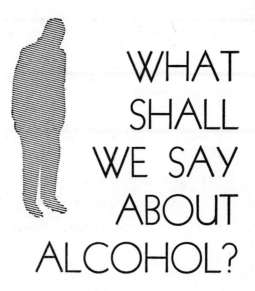

WHAT SHALL WE SAY ABOUT ALCOHOL?

ABINGDON PRESS   ⑆   NEW YORK · NASHVILLE

WHAT SHALL WE SAY ABOUT ALCOHOL?

Library of Congress Catalog Card Number: 60-6931

Scripture quotations unless otherwise noted are
from the Revised Standard Version of the Bible
and are copyright 1946 and 1952 by the Division of Christian Education of the National
Council of the Churches of Christ in the U.S.A.

Scripture quotations from J. B. Phillips, *The
New Testament in Modern English*, are used
by permission of The Macmillan Company and
Geoffrey Bles Ltd.

SET UP, PRINTED, AND BOUND BY THE
PARTHENON PRESS, AT NASHVILLE,
TENNESSEE, UNITED STATES OF AMERICA

DEDICATION

To my wife, **Lila Maud,** whose consecrated optimism
has made our service together a constant pageant of joy.

INTRODUCTION

❦ A DISTINGUISHED CLERGYMAN ONCE DECLARED THAT the world in which we live is too dangerous for anything but the truth and too small for anything but brotherhood. In an era that is motivated by half-truths and half-lies, one must discriminate lest one fall victim to what is neither wholly false nor yet the truth.

Our society faces a great growing moral challenge if it is to remain a free society. If we are unwilling as a people to accept a certain discipline, to admit our responsibility for others as for self, to rediscover the real purpose and direction of our existence, we shall not be free.

The most decisive issue before the American people today is the quality of the moral response they will make to the problems they face. One of those problems, and related to many others, is social drinking. This is a malignancy which tends to destroy personal as well as national freedom. Our nation under God will not survive half drunk and half sober.

We have temporized with this menace and refused to face the theological and ethical implications of self-indulgence. There are some growing signs of sobriety in the nation. For such trends we are grateful, but let us not underestimate the strength of the foe we face or the magnitude of the conflict we are in.

Caradine R. Hooton, General Secretary of the Methodist Board of Temperance, has for many years been in the forefront of this battle for sobriety. His keen, intuitive mind has seen the problem and seen it whole. His case against alcohol is made on every front—theological, ethical, and moral. With the skill of an attorney and yet with the winsomeness of a man committed to Jesus Christ, he pleads his case. He knows the tragedy of moral decline and its social consequences. Not alone the nature of alcohol, but the nature of man engages his mind and heart.

Here is a book which with a passion born of inner rectitude indicts the alcohol industry, and with a passion born of the love of God offers help for the helpless. The minister and the teacher will find this volume useful as they reach for a verdict, and the layman will read it for encouragement along life's way. To all who will make the moral response, I commend this book of suggested solutions to problems for which there is no easy answer.

John Wesley Lord

Bishop of The Methodist Church
Boston Area

FOREWORD

❧ THE PASTOR'S TELEPHONE RINGS. IT IS TWO O'CLOCK on Sunday morning. A familiar voice says, "Please come to the police station. A man has been killed. They are holding me. Drinking and driving is the charge. What can I do?"

A husband comes to see the minister. He must have help in problems for which he has no solution. His wife is becoming an alcoholic and the children are drifting away. Can the church supply a quick answer?

A prospective new member asks, "What's the harm in a little drink or two?" Another wants to know, "How can you make people good by legislation?" The questions are many; good answers are few.

The uses of alcohol have involved every parish in complex problems for which there is no easy answer. Drinking has become such an enigma in modern life that pastors, teachers, and citizens are sometimes baffled for adequate solutions.

Preferring subjects less controversial and more conducive to peace of mind, churchmen sometimes seek escape from temperance lessons and sermons. They are like Abe Lincoln's farmer friend who was confronted by a tree stump too big to pull, too wet to burn. "I'll tell you how I got rid of that stump," volunteered the farmer. "I plowed around it."

Everywhere today thoughtful people are troubled over the magnitude of the drinking menace. They are disturbed, too, because of the oversimplifications by some and the awkward approaches of others who try in vain to untangle the complicated effects of inebriety. Many are puzzled over best methods of prevention.

Seeing that drinking does not satisfy the deeper thirsts of people, how can leaders persuade persons to try disciplines that do? Perhaps some know in advance where "temperance preaching" will come out, but is there not keen desire for a demonstration of how it can get into the life of people? Many moderns will welcome a series of good messages on alcohol. They have tired of diatribes against drinkers which have too long cut off effective communication.

Everybody is impressed when some government official says, "More secrets about American security have been leaked by the loose-tongued in liquor taverns than through any other source of information." But are churchmen disturbed over the report that more people today go to bartenders than to Christians for counseling and guidance?

What answers do the churches have for critical needs of the cocktail community? Because preachers, teachers, and parents do have difficulties with the unsolved problems of drinking and abstinence, this book offers approaches and procedures which we believe will be challenging and helpful.

It is hoped that leaders may find in these pages some ideas for constructive thought and counseling that will lead to new life in Christ for many. We believe that all people have the right, without undue pressures:

> to enjoy liberty from abnormal inducements to drink;
>
> to experience healthy growth of body, mind, and soul;
>
> to achieve maturity without manipulation;
>
> to realize complete mental, social, and spiritual fulfillment.

The task of the churches, in keeping persons sensitive to these high privileges, is to point all men always to the Great Teacher who offers his Spirit as our stimulus.

Through him many interfaith activities are bringing all Christians closer together in opposition to alcohol and in support of positive approaches and Christian objectives. Areas of agreement among churches are now on more solid foundations than ever before. Differences have to do with degrees of rejection of social drinking and disciplines for the prevention of alcoholism.

There is a marked contemporary trend away from alcohol itself as a solution. But many are still without knowledge of alternatives for adequate living. Too many remain in abysmal darkness concerning damage that comes from occasional drinking. Your knowledge can become the light that may keep many from being hurt.

There is no easy answer for the complicated problems of alcohol, but your effort may spark the search for him who is the Light and the Life men really want.

CARADINE R. HOOTON

CONTENTS

13

I

THE CHURCH HAS NEW APPROACHES

*"We should be willing to be both vegetarians
and teetotalers if by doing otherwise we should
impede a brother's progress in the faith."*
(Rom. 14:21 Phillips.)

Respond, O Church! This is the hour
To make thy ministry complete;
Christ waits to furnish thee the power
To lift the city to His feet.[1]

The church has always been the greatest foe of the
liquor business. It is still the best friend of alcohol's victims. But are we effectively communicating this concern to people who need our help?

The alcohol problem is stupendous in size. It challenges the strength of the church, the very life of its
people. How can the church measure up to its unique
opportunity for creative service to people with a mind-set
for drinking?

One of the great difficulties has been to formulate a
program and devise terminologies that people will understand and accept. Another problem was how to

break through the glamorization of social drinking with sobering facts about the uses of alcohol and Christian responsibility!

In a large group of church leaders gathered to discuss the possibilities for a church-wide emphasis on the problems of alcohol, one asked, "Can there be anything really new in an approach to temperance education?"

The answer here is easy enough to understand but most difficult to communicate. Some people get lost when the temperance issue is discussed from any viewpoint that does not focus solely upon "prohibition." This good word has become a red flag. But there are other needs that must first be considered.

A Virginia pastor was trying to be faithful to all needs of his two-point charge. Seeking to serve both congregations on the same Sunday, he sent out this notice: "There will be preaching in the west end at 11:00 A.M., preaching in the east end at 3:00 P.M., and babies will be baptized at both ends."

If we are going to be realistic, it is necessary to cultivate the people who like prohibition and find ways to communicate with minds that are closed to temperance. There are new approaches that are accomplishing these two ends. Old terminologies since repeal have not inspired creative action in the modern world. The opposition has developed new strategies that must be countered with better skills and methods of education.

With the loss of national prohibition, dry forces were thrown into utter confusion. The churches constituted "a minority protest" against bad customs and practices which had become commonly accepted. The licensed industry was now exercising its most powerful influence over the processes of government and social change. Could there be enough ingenuity, imagination, and resourcefulness among churchmen to successfully reverse the trend?

Following prayer and consultations with a host of concerned leaders, new light began to dawn. Formerly there had been much activity in a sustained fight against alcohol. But action without education was labeled "fanaticism." Experience had long taught that education without action is sterility. What would be winsomely new and at the same time acceptably true in the area of temperance education and action?

First, a *positive attitude*. This would suggest a proclamation of the positive benefits of Christian living instead of a negative condemnation of alcohol and drinkers.

The whole idea of temperance had fallen out of character into caricature. The very mention of the word had come to be associated with types of frantic reformers who want to force their thought and manner of life upon all others.

Christians are not people who always speak negatively, nor are they persons who spend their days only in opposition to alcohol, gambling, prostitution, and the like. The Christian church has a clear-sounding, affirmative truth to proclaim. Conditions not only warrant but demand frequent and forthright denunciations of evil. This means everything that obviously weakens character and deters the progress of cultural development.

17

While we have always been opposed to promiscuous uses of alcohol in beverage form, let no one think that condemnation is all that a Christian church has to offer. Primarily, our message is positive truth, rather than punitive criticism. Our effort is more concerned with building character than blasting creatures. We abhor evils but understand evildoers. We war against the sin as we try to win the sinner.

The new approach is to present alcoholic beverages as antithetical to wholesome Christian living. Undoubtedly, abstinence is a desirable practice which makes possible a better understanding of God, a deeper appreciation of our fellow man, a more constructive social interrelatedness and satisfying investment of life.

We make war against the liquor business because its product and program are in conflict with best human interests. At the same time we point out better ways of spending money, using time, and even converting machinery into the production of useful commodities.

The second outstanding feature is a study of *motivations*—understanding why people drink.

Once our chief emphasis was to destroy the liquor traffic. Toward that end prohibition is effective as long as people want to support it. It is one of the potent instruments of legal protection which undoubtedly results in large benefits to people, but at best it is only a means to the primary objective of Christian faith and action.

The larger purpose of any legislation is to prevent damage to human personality while fortifying society for educational advance. But working through and beyond these techniques must be the compulsion of love which inspires the treatment of root causes of individual and social delinquencies.

Motivations for abstinence and prohibition must also result in Christian disciplines that lead to orderly social togetherness. Instead of looking solely at the bad in others we seek to discover the potential good in all. Not content merely to deal with problems, we insist upon understanding people.

Why do people drink? Are not the uses of alcoholic beverages symptoms of deeper needs which are not being more effectively met otherwise? Instead of merely damning the drink, we seek an understanding of drives that, after all, can only be satisfied by something better than alcohol.

In a study of motivations there is also need to build the case for abstinence around positive benefits rather than potential dangers.

It is exceedingly important for moderns to understand why people reach for the cocktail glass. They need to know that the church has far better remedies for what ails persons than the social circle can supply. But if we expect to make much headway toward abstinence, this must be demonstrated in gracious alcohol-free living and through attractive alternatives for intoxicants. Furthermore, while alcohol is a factor in many types of misbehavior, there are always other elements in character deficiency that need to be understood and corrected.

The third innovation in temperance education is *the skillful use of scientific facts.* Modern laboratories have, through extensive research, developed an abundance of basic data that can be most helpful in promoting abstinence. There is no longer any excuse for unrealistic speculation about certain effects of drinking. The provable damage of ethyl alcohol to the thought processes, the nervous system, and muscular reaction is enough, when properly presented, to discourage experiments with drinking.

These effects are shown to be a direct reversal of the learning process. Without going through the normal routine of digestion, beverage alcohol, ingested, makes its way by absorption into the blood stream, and immediately invades the brain centers. Acting as an anesthetic, it puts to sleep the top intelligence area of the mind and reduces rational self-control. Inasmuch as it requires several hours for oxidation to expel this depressant element from the system, many forms of damage may result. Loss of reasoning power makes for irresponsible action that retards growth and often occasions grief.

This affords teachers an opportunity to move into the hygienic benefits of nonalcoholic beverages, and the social advantages found in alternatives for intoxicants.

Coupled with accurate presentations of fact is the need for strengthening faith. This suggests a fourth emphasis in the modern approach, viz., *giving theological and ethical support to temperance education.* Scientific knowledge should stimulate stewardship concern, but some who are best informed are guilty of the worst performances. The pattern for good leadership can be developed only by persons who grow in faith as they gain knowledge of facts.

When the Bible says, "Wine is a mocker, strong drink a brawler; And whosoever erreth thereby is not wise" (A.S.V.), can we prove that it is true physically, socially, and spiritually? Both facts and faith are ready with the answer, Yes.

The Scriptures are quite clear in a general condemnation of all purposes and practices that separate men from God or encourage persons to settle for less than the Father intended his children should be. The Bible opposes drunkenness; it stands for disciplines that build character and glorify Christ. There are implications that intoxicants are to be administered by prescription only, or as an anodyne in cases of extreme necessity.

The ethical reasons for abstinence are far more conclusive than employment of proof-texts for or against drinking. Further along we shall examine passages and principles that inveigh against intemperance and recommend abstinence.

Let us come now to another important point of approach, the fifth new element in alcohol education: the *communication of truth in more meaningful terms.* Characteristic of too many sincere temperance advocates is the tendency both to moralize and to judge. People resent threats and reject the pietistic approach. Sincerity is not the sole ingredient of persuasiveness.

Individuals and audiences close their minds to initial suggestions that "drinking is wrong" or to assertions that "alcohol is a poison." A better beginning is to relate

21

familiar facts with which the other or others have some connection on the assumption that they have a concern and are capable of making decisions.

Moderns can understand us better when we talk about drinking and driving, public health problems related to alcohol, efficiency in industry, or alcohol-related arrests. They respect intelligent efforts to present scientific truths about the risks of drinking ethyl alcohol as contrasted with beneficial uses of commercial alcohol.

The communicator commands attention when he accepts the listener as equally interested in studying, facing, and solving the problems that challenge extraordinary citizenship concern. A passing look at some of these social ills can effect mental agreements that will soon make possible the more specific look at other effects of drinking.

When the "listeners'" minds are open, the speaker may lead on to the more serious aspects of the moral principles involved. Overt verbalization will thus increase the rate of acceptance of verbal material. This calm reasoning registers a marked gain in learning efficiency. And it does more. It enables the leader to carry individuals of the group through the various stages of disbelief to some regard for the leader's viewpoint. The art of persuasion consists also in projecting these new understandings into special undertakings for the benefit of others. Effective communication can thus result in efficient crusading.

Appealing now to open minds, the temperance leader may stress commitments which before would have been impossible. Dr. Robert S. Clemmons says in his *Dynamics of Christian Adult Education*,

This is an age of communication. We possess more powerful gadgets to transmit ideas than any nation in history. Radio, television, the press, pour out daily an undigestible quantity of ideas, notions, and opinions. Yet we seem to understand each other less. Why? Is communication more than the powerful transmission of ideas? . . . Communication is a two-way street.[2]

Barriers of anxiety, mobility, irrelevancy, and confusion need to be overcome. When we demonstrate a real concern for others we put ourselves in a position to effectively share the whole truth about alcohol's being opposed to the spirit of Christ. Only when we break down the noxious barricades that shut off all too many people from the truth can these people be convinced that alcoholic beverages ridicule, despise, deceive, and disappoint men in their quest for life.

True understanding of the Bible and of the ethical necessity for sober service projects temperance education beyond hopeful theory into helpful practice.

New curricular materials now being offered by many churches include the latest and best scientific and spiritual approaches to an understanding of the complex problem of alcohol. They also inculcate principles of Christian concern which promise a redemption of society from the ruin of alcoholism.

Current church-wide studies on the problems of alcohol can become one of America's greatest opportunities for church extension, missionary expansion, and evangelistic endeavor. With timely information about alcohol, temperance leaders might help others come to the sound conclusion which Sir Wilfred Grenfell reached. He said, "When I first made up my mind that I wanted to be as perfect a citizen as I could, the first thing I did was swear off all alcoholic beverages."

No amount of temperance education is complete until people are led to apply the threefold test of all Christian behavior, namely, to remember who they are; to remember that they are not their own; and to remember where they are going. As stewards we are to give account of ourselves while answering for the fate of others.

Knowing that there are effective new ways of getting acceptance of temperance truths, let us remember that

> The greatest church in all the land,
> With wealth and power in its control,
> Holds naught but ashes in its hand
> Unless it guards the city's soul.
> What means a great and granite pile
> To Christian worship set apart,
> If city streets, mile after mile,
> Feel not the throbbing of its heart? [3]

---

[1] Phillips Brooks.

[2] Robert S. Clemmons, *Dynamics of Christian Adult Education* (Nashville: Abingdon Press, 1958), p. 78.

[3] Phillips Brooks.

24

II

WHO AM I?

"If . . . you cut the nerve of your instinctive actions by obeying the Spirit, you are on the way to real living." (Rom. 8:13 Phillips.)

The church has more than new approaches. It has true appreciation for persons. Made up of people like you and me, its members should be growing toward maturity. In no other way can we hope to deal successfully with the alcohol problem.

The Christian's example of abstinence and concern will become the church's most respected preceptor. But because people are imperfect and the effects of alcohol vary, there is no easy solution to the drinking dilemma. If we are to provide the right answer, it will be necessary to start where we are with a study of who we are, as persons.

Alcohol can have a direct bearing upon what I am, what I may become, and how I relate to God and the world in which I live. Human behavior is affected by two types of pressure: internal and external. These forces have a determining influence upon the growth of personality, the development of social conscience, and the acceptance of responsibility.

A wrong choice in Eden was the beginning of a succession of human failures that revealed the need of divine deliverance. In the struggle for mastery of his work, man developed a withering sense of inadequacy that intensified his quest for help. His problem has always been to curb his cave-man inclinations and to harness his instincts for survival. His intuitions and his capacity for becoming something better than he is have led from abortive experiments in self-control to high adventures in social reform.

In the depths of our nature there is the potential savage. Dr. Frederick Brown Harris, in "Spires of the Spirit" says, "There is a zoo in you." This is probably so. We do have such expressions as "sly as a fox," "eats like a pig," "drinks like a fish," "stubborn as a mule," "proud as a peacock," "fierce as a lion." When man's bestiality overcomes his spirituality, the devastation is as terrible as that left by the escaped gorilla in Poe's "The Murders in the Rue Morgue."

Who am I? invites further exploration. For I am a tripartite combination of mind, body, and spirit.

As mind, I consist of an "id," an "ego," and a "super-ego." Psychologists say the id is a storehouse for all my energy, the reservoir for basic drives. The psychiatrist who asked a student to define the id, got this reply: "It is a substance which is soluble in alcohol." The thinking of this punster was in line with the assertion of a current statesman who said, "A man who gets himself enslaved to intoxicants is a plain idiot."

In this basement of animalistic drives are found the instinct for self-preservation and the desire to be comfortable. Sorokin insists that in our "sensate culture" the determination to coddle the desires of the senses is a number-one concern of society. Are you not urged to "travel in comfort," "enjoy yourself," and remember that "where there's life, there's Bud"?

Aldous Huxley wrote an essay entitled, "Wanted: A New Pleasure." In it he suggests that

the only new pleasure would be derived from the invention of a new drug which would provide a harmless substitute for alcohol. . . . If this heavenly world-transforming drug were of such a kind that we could wake up next morning with a clear head and undamaged constitution, our problem would be solved and earth would become a paradise.

Maybe this explains the invitation of the paganistic ad which made its recent appearance in a metropolitan paper. It read,

"May we suggest champagne for your Sunday breakfast? Orange juice may be adequate for week-day breakfasts. But comes Sunday, you owe yourself a little of that feeling of ineffable luxury that comes only from a bottle of champagne before Sunday noon. A couple of glasses of this beverage with your late Sunday breakfast and you will spend the rest of the day with your feet planted firmly in the clouds."

27

Could this be a match to the church that features "delightful air-conditioning, foam rubber seats, and a service that won't go over 59 minutes"?

In an effort to displace "reality-orientation" with "pleasure-realization," advertising engineers appeal to man's ever-present instinct to be comfortable. They capitalize on the childish disposition betrayed by the small girl who said,

> I had a little tea party this after-
>   noon at three
> 'Twas very small—just three
>   guests in all—
> I, Myself, and Me.
>
> Myself ate all the sandwiches
>   While I drank all the tea
> 'Twas also I who ate the pie
>   And passed the cake to Me.[1]

But "is everybody happy" when they only get what the ads say their ids demand? Fortunately the "will-to-pleasure" idea can be superceded by what modern psychotherapists call the "will to meaning." In this generation, confronted with the sociological triad of automation, aged people, and juvenile delinquency, among other problems, many persons develop an inner vacuum that needs special treatment. The resultant state of boredom, otherwise known as a sort of Sunday neurosis or after-cocktail depression, can only be overcome by the injection of spiritual vitamins in the blood stream.

Hunger for pleasure is the escape from one's existential frustration; but whenever we are trying to take refuge in intoxication to drug the inner void, we are neglecting the essence of human existence—that is: to direct oneself to the realm of values and meaning, to devote oneself to the actualization of specific values.[2]

Not only so, but the drinker is playing Russian roulette with himself. Persistence in the use of alcohol is like holding a nine-bullet pistol to the head. Eight of the cylinders contain potential powder burns, but one chamber is loaded with a lethal shot that floors the victim with alcoholism.

People drink because in life's basement they get lonely, develop emptiness, and long for satisfaction. Here they think too much of the nominative "I," the possessive "Mine," and the objective "Me." Gerald O. McCulloh tells of the woman who asked a preacher to come and pray for her dying mother. He found a pitiful prostitute in a smelly room, with a crucifix above the bed. On the nearby table was a bottle of rum. The bottle was in rapport, but the crucifix was not. And yet, the presence of the figure and the minister's prayer of faith were indications that in all people there is a desire to be better than they are.

This hope is enhanced by the operation of the ego. Every rational being has the capacity to perceive the bodily drives, the disposition to satisfy "wants," and the ability to make evaluations. He can sense, with Phillips Brooks, that "the first secret of all effective and happy living is a true reverence for the mystery and greatness of your human nature, for the living things which you and your brethren are, in simply being men."

There is something in each of us that can ultimately say, "I am not going to let anything master me." But the desire to achieve distinction may overpower our better judgment. Short cuts to a personal sense of importance lead all too often to the nearest cocktail glass. Alcohol does, indeed, palliate certain needs that will be discussed in connection with motivations for drinking. It never satisfies!

Every rational person also has the potential capacity to evaluate activities that relate to moral values. This is the superego. Here is the area of conscience that may become "good" or "bad" through association and training. By the process of rationalization, one may angle himself into acceptance of second-best things for meeting bodily demands. He may also succeed in resisting evil pressures.

What I really am is determined finally by the aliveness and responsiveness of my spirit to the highest and best values in life. John Wesley said, "One design we are to pursue to the end of time—the enjoyment of God in time and eternity. Desire other things so far as they tend to this. Love the creature as it leads to the Creator." [3]

This suggests consideration of *What I become.* All men are what they are because of heritage, environment, and choice. These decisive elements in human destiny challenge one's ability to visualize what he ought to be. We are inclined to look for characters or dream of patterns that represent an ideal worthy of emulation. Depth psychologists often help or hinder with their efforts to influence decisions which one would not normally make.[4]

And how may I properly relate to God and others? This is life's greatest question. One may be a kind of "saint" among men, but he will never find satisfaction without God. For until he is in proper rapport with God, he can never fully meet responsibilities to men. This extraordinary "power to become" is completely realized only when one acts upon the truth that "it is in Christ Jesus that full life is reached." Drinkers are temporarily content with being; Christians are satisfied only with becoming.

Men are more than body, mind, and spirit. Possessing self-consciousness, world-awareness, and soul-relationship with God, they become children of the heavenly Father. They may develop concern for all fellow beings. Such men can say with Roy Z. Kemp:

> Thrice happy am I in His love
> And this to Him I owe
> I love Him, and my friend in Him
> And for His sake, my foe.[5]

This generation needs nothing more than Christian men who are concerned with lifting the world to a new plane of reverence for God, respect for self, and responsibility for others. To this end everyone should pray with Hamilton Wright Mabie:

Send someone, Lord, to love the best that is in me,
  And to accept nothing less from me;
To demand everything from me for my own sake.[6]

Without concern for personal growth and the welfare of others we would be like the man in the parable of the rich fool who wanted only his ease in eating, drinking, and making merry. Jesus called him foolish because he forgot that he had a soul to account for.

At his best man is a soul. It is for this reason that alcohol is a major enemy. The man who drinks always runs the risk of damnation both here and hereafter. Alcohol does more than blur the brain: it disturbs the nervous system, upsets the digestive and circulatory operation, and blinds the spiritual insights. Drinking stymies achievement, as it drugs the mind and depresses bodily functions. Alcohol defeats life's larger purposes by supplying inadequate "satisfactions" which arrest true progress and halt creative pursuits. Reliance upon the "glass crutch" results in immaturity and ultimate alienation from God.

Called to freedom, abstaining Christians may say, "Thanks be to God who leads us, wherever we are, on his own triumphant way and makes our knowledge of him to spread throughout the world like a lovely perfume!" (II Cor. 2:14 Phillips.)

The image of the man of distinction puts me in the middle, and I soon become bored with myself. However attractive it is otherwise made to appear, alcohol produces delusions. Christ provides deliverance by transforming desires. He represents the pattern of what men, deep down, think they ought to be.

With the spirit of Christ in the heart, we are on the way to victorious living. This involves more than personal enjoyment. It fills us with a spiritual plenty that overflows into the lives of others. Its contagion excites the kind of concern that becomes a blessing to others.

[1] Jessica Nelson North MacDonald, "The Three Guests." Reprinted by permission of author.

[2] Viktor E. Frankl.

[3] John Wesley, "The Use of Money" (J. D. Booth, York), 4th ed., pp. 128-29.

[4] Vance Packard, The Hidden Persuaders (New York: David McKay Co., Inc., 1957).

[5] Roy Z. Kemp, "Trinity," The Christian Century, January 7, 1959. Copyright 1959 Christian Century Foundation. Reprinted by permission.

[6] Hamilton Wright Mabie. Used by permission of The Christian Century.

III

WHO ARE THEY?

*"Be sober, be vigilant; because your adversary
the devil, as a roaring lion, walketh about, seeking whom he may devour: Whom resist stead-
fast in the faith."* (I Pet. 5:8-9 K.J.V.)

Enemies of social progress are not always easy to iden-
tify. Chief among the organized forces at war against
character growth and community welfare is the legalized
alcohol industry. U.S. Brewers Foundation now lists
more than four hundred "associate members" of this
gigantic pressure bloc. Christians who have for years
been fighting the liquor traffic are confronted with new
opposition by these allied interests.

Some marketers of intoxicants focus upon the personality they think I want to be—poised, influential, successful, distinctive. They know that all persons react
according to character and environment, and by subtle
suggestion they attempt to mold men to their own image
of "important personalities." Therefore, each individual
and all social strata become targets for the skills of the
commercial marksmen.

In order to sell alcoholic beverages they employ depth

psychologists who major in motivational research. Not content to work on persons as they are, these social engineers mold images of what they think potential customers would like to be. They create highly appealing "personalities," even for products that are essentially undistinctive. By skillful subliminal suggestion, the TV viewer, for example, is gradually impressed with a sense of the importance which even he may acquire by consuming a particular brand.

These psychologists take advertising far beyond the skills of presenting products on their basic merits. By association, they create an illogical situation to inspire both use of unwanted commodities and a sense of loyalty to particular brands that have no distinctive quality. The effort is to develop an illogical devotion to a product or practice by creating some acceptance or differentiation in the mind.

The "wonderful image" idea has been successfully employed in the selling of cigarettes, automobiles, soaps, and alcoholic beverages. There are cases of men who could, when hypnotized, repeat word for word ads they had read earlier which had stuck in their minds.[1] Advertisers are taking full advantage of the old psychological truism that "whatever gets your imagination gets you."

They have gone all out to "make beer belong," to turn every social into a cocktail party, and to pressure every family into gleeful acceptance of alcohol. Americans are told that to click with the crowd they must learn how to handle their liquor.

As a part of the theory of "belongingness," advertisers

of intoxicants insist that people who want fun find it by drinking together. Falling for this "device to create the atmosphere of a picnic," many have conformed to the convivial "we feeling" with regrets. In polls recently conducted, a majority of drinkers attributed their first uses of alcoholic beverages to appetizing advertisements and to social pressure, in that order.

When the well-known "family-life series" of colorful ads represented beer as the commonly accepted beverage of "most young adults," a Nashville, Tennessee, housewife vigorously protested. Two days later, after she had written a letter to the brewing advertiser, an official of the company flew in from St. Louis to persuade her that she was wrong. After extended conversation with her in which her convictions prevailed, the brewer went home and withdrew the misleading ad.

Can anyone successfully contend that families who drink together, stay together? Ceremonies that have their beginnings in highballs usually end in heartaches. Let us hope that America will not lag behind the Soviet Union in putting a collective ban on the kind of drinking that too soon reduces people to mere puppets.

In the face of pressures to use alcohol, how many think independently? In the search for happiness, men are made to believe that alcohol is an essential ingredient of good entertainment. All references point to the "cocktail" dress, table, lounge, hour, party, bar, or what-have-you. Liquor interests now provide carefully trained public relations experts, hostesses, campus pushers, and party directors—anything—to inject alcohol into planned dinners, receptions, and social functions.

They are now deceiving the people through the use of another reprehensible strategem. Remember World Health Organization's factual filmstrip, "To Your Health"? It is an unbiased exposé of some of the consequences of drinking which everyone has a right to know. To offset the film's effect and fortify its own appeal to potential consumers, the whisky trust immediately produced an elaborate moving picture in color which glorifies drinking. To complete the deception it has taken advantage of the popularity of "To Your Health" by naming its more elaborate production "To Your Very Good Health."

Washington's largest newspaper recently carried an editorial that caricatures many Christians as "temperance zealots" and "intransigent drys." Interspersing the news columns, of course, were many conspicuous liquor ads! In the next issue of this paper the chief judge of Municipal Court made an eloquent appeal for "help in treating alcoholics." He suggested "broader sentencing authority, housing for homeless drunks, a bigger staff at the Alcoholic Rehabilitation Clinic, and more court probation officers to handle heavy case loads."

The fifty thousand seriously incapacitated people in the District of Columbia are only a small percentage of the population who are being hurt by careless drinking. The five million alcoholics of the nation and the rapid increase of problem drinkers pose a major health problem everywhere.[2] In this connection we should be constantly reminded of two facts: that at least one in every nine who begins to drink becomes a problem drinker, and that science knows no way of predetermining which ones will succumb. Educators, officers, ministers, and undertakers know that what happens to the "other eight" is often more tragic than alcoholic sickness.

In traffic accidents we kill approximately forty thousand persons each year. The National Safety Council now says that from 30 per cent to 50 per cent of these are casualties in which drinking (not drunkenness) is a factor. According to reliable statistics, the total of these killings constitutes a larger number of casualties than we have suffered in war.[3]

This does not include injuries, property damage, and economic loss. It does not take into account the nameless and shameful immoralities which are more grievous than those incidents that hit the headlines. Alcohol and crime were characterized by Senator Estes Kefauver as inextricably tied together.[4]

On the same date of the *Post's* unfortunate editorial, a very tragic accident occurred in the Washington Zoo. It was the first of its kind in sixty-three years of the Zoo's history. A little two-year-old girl who broke loose from her grandfather's hand was dragged into a cage by hungry lions and decapitated. The newspapers, radio, and television featured the story for two days, and everybody was shocked. After the tragedy, the lion cages were shut and the killer was destroyed.

But little or nothing is said about the catastrophes that result from the uninterrupted operations of another

38

"roaring lion (that) walketh about, seeking whom he may devour." This is a familiar figure of speech used in the First Epistle of Peter to describe uncaged activities of an adversary too seldom recognized as the devil. In our day he has shed his long tail, sharp tusks, and forked talons. The only remaining horns are those used for sounding his own praises. This adversary now appears in full dress suit as a suave and most persuasive personality. Claiming only "men of distinction" as products of its operation, this modern foe seeks recognition as a friend.

Paying back to the government only a part of its exhorbitant "take" in the form of taxes, the alcohol business demands special privileges and expects public approval. In an effort to maintain popular tolerance it champions every possible benevolence under the guise of brotherly concern. Yet many of our charitable institutions may trace the largest per cent of their troubles to the hurtful effects of somebody's drinking.

The government has often treated this slinking creature as a sacred cow. But the records in some states prove that for every dollar received from liquor revenue, the government pays out an average of six dollars for enforcement, damage, and care.[5]

It is the sad reality of world-wide want that renders support of the alcohol industry so insupportable. Alcoholic beverages do not contain sufficient food or drug value to warrant the waste of natural resources required for production. In his book *That They Might Have Bread*, Robert Britain contends that for the price of only two years of America's liquor bill ($20,000,000,000) the

U.S.A. could supply resources that would feed the world for many years to come.

This elevation of profits above principle in face of naked starvation constitutes a most sinister threat to world peace. One of the most difficult hurdles between us and international good will is our lackadaisical submission to the overlordship of liquor.

It is obvious that the alcohol business intends to sell more intoxicants to an ever-expanding range of potential customers, including young people, women, and children. How can people be protected from the constant assaults that are made upon homes, schools, clubs, churches, the reading public, and the millions who view television? The answer is not easy.

Great preachers of many generations have cried aloud against this business as an unjustifiable "traffic." Said John Wesley:

All who sell liquors in the common way to any that will buy are poisoners general. . . . It is amazing that the preparing or selling this poison should be permitted, I shall not say in any Christian country but in any civilized state.[6]

Harry Emerson Fosdick sums it up for moderns when he says:

The liquor traffic is for everything we are against, and against everything we are for. At the heart of the Christian conscience of this country there is a conviction—make up your mind to it—that the liquor traffic and the Christian gospel stand for two diverse and contradictory conceptions of personal and social life.[7]

History corroborates these conclusions.

What the great statesman Isaiah said of alcohol's subversive influence in his day seems applicable to effects of drinking today. Turn to Isaiah 5 and read that "Hell hath enlarged herself"—with help from the handlers of liquor. Our generation surely needs once more to reckon with Habakkuk's "Woe unto him that giveth his neighbor drink, that puttest the bottle to him, and makest him drunken also." (Hab. 2:15 K.J.V.)

This is not just a concern for ministers. Facing the alcohol problem and defending people against invasions by the alcohol industry are specific citizenship responsibilities of major importance. There are those who think the simple solution would be to shut off the source of our trouble by outlawing the trade. This, of course, is an illusory answer for which men have found no easy implementation.

But how may Christians protect themselves and others against the depredations of these allied liquor interests? Let us consider three strategies:

First, let Christians be sober! This means literally, "Be free from every form of mental and spiritual drunkenness, from excess, passion, confusion." Moffatt says it means, "Keep cool!"

It has sometimes been tritely said that the alcohol problem could be solved if churchmen would quit drinking. This obviously is an oversimplification. Among

America's 57,000,000 users of alcoholic beverages there are admittedly too many church members who drink. Let us be thankful that at least 45,000,000 mature persons in the U.S.A. never use alcohol in beverage form. Let us so live that other millions of children and youth will never learn to like intoxicants.

All those who drink undoubtedly weaken their witness, impair their physical and financial strength, and give sanction and support to one of the church's greatest foes. If churchmen would positively abstain and make the Christian religion attractive, outsiders would soon be led to amend their ways. Many liquor stores would automatically go out of business. In due time the number of saloons, now 480,000 (including grocery store permits) might be at least reduced to the number of churches, 240,000.

A University of Pennsylvania student believed that a Christian should be sober in all circumstances. Asked by his imbibing fraternity brothers if he expected to drink the spiked punch they would find at the forthcoming wedding party, he politely said, "No." When they wanted to argue the point, he suggested that the hostess would, in all good taste, likely provide nonintoxicants for all abstainers. "But if she doesn't, would you, by refusing a drink, pose as better than Christ who made wine at Cana?" In winsome reply, the heckled student said, "No, I'll always drink anything Jesus made out of water."

Second, let Christians be vigilant. Peter never forgot that when Christ needed them most the disciples went to sleep. Now he admonished watchfulness.

Purveyors of liquor and those who profit from its sale and consumption spare no effort in pushing the trade. Offering increased revenue to communities, added employment to labor, higher salaries to teachers, support of charities, they plan long-range schemes designed to soften resistance to their operations. While our leaders are preoccupied with important character-building projects and the promotion of better human relationships, they are "pressuring" legislatures and organizations that can give prestige and power to the liquor business.

Vigilance is needed to offset these subtle infiltrations. It may take the form of electing good men to office, encouraging better law enforcement, informing people of the facts about drinking, and making alternatives for alcohol more appetizing and alluring. Active and vigorous opposition to all sanctions so persistently sought by the liquor business must be matched by Christian alertness to human needs and ingenuity in supplying proper solutions.

There is a fight on against foes. They want to sell their products. We want to serve people. Compromise would be catastrophe.

Third, resist this adversary, standing firm in the faith. Firmness does not mean scurrilous attack upon those who disagree with us. Nor does our faith imply that resistance must always presuppose unfaithfulness by those who have another viewpoint. The type of opposition supplied by some reformers has not won friends and favorably influenced people. Culture patterns are not changed for the better by fanatics.

43

Here is the good fight of a faith that always demands and gets respect: "They always win who side with God. To them no cause is lost."

The personal and social damage that results from drinking and the half-truths of advertising can no longer be discounted or ignored. But the public needs more knowledge of the superior benefits of abstinence and sound legal controls, so that major attention can be focused here.

The alcohol industry and its allies cannot be depended upon to make any voluntary reforms. Nor will outmoded temperance techniques effect the desired change. But there are positive ways of establishing sobriety in American life. The liquor industry itself is toying with the idea of conversion of business and machinery into more constructive uses.

Meanwhile, we can make our own "product" more potent. Knowledge of scientific facts is still inadequate. But some who know the truth about alcohol are slaves to its tortures. It takes more than facts: men need faith. To help develop this capacity there is need for contact with true Christians. Abstainers can make the alcohol-free way of life so desirable that people will be drawn more easily than driven to accept its superb advantages.

The churches can become such amiable centers of fellowship that people will prefer them to the cocktail circuit. When individuals find a new interest in Christ they learn to enjoy fellowship with his people. They in turn experience a new thrill in bringing friends into this orbit of purposeful living.

The conversion that would "save" the alcohol business is a transformation of motive and machinery. It is often objected that restraints against the liquor trade work hardships on employment.[8] But there is little thought given to the distress that comes to many through the displacements caused by drinking. How many are unemployed because of the unbridled operation of the liquor business!

There is need of distilleries. Commercial uses of alcohol offer unlimited demands for full-scale production. Only 20 per cent of distilled spirits are now used for commercial purposes. Let us encourage every movement toward those uses of people and property which would benefit humanity.

Is there any justification for the continued operation of these plants for manufacturing alcoholic beverages? No. The alcohol industry, as at present constituted, has been tried and found wanting. The courageous young director of America's most famous scientific school of alcohol studies said one day to this writer's staff, "The licensed liquor business has no worthy service motivation —its sole aim is profit."

Abraham Lincoln went even farther. He advocated abolition of the liquor traffic and would bring new liberties to the people through "a temperance revolution." [9]

Students of a great denominational university found a unique way to demonstrate their love of humanity and loyalty to truth. A brewer's big horses were coming to town. This team had been everywhere diverting attention from the destructiveness of the alcohol traffic to the stateliness of trained thoroughbreds. The students decorated huge trucks and followed the beer wagon on parade. The gruesome display of crashed cars, damaged property, and injured people represented very true pictures of the end results of drinking. Using tomato catsup and red paint, these students cleverly presented such a bloody reminder of the damage done to people by alcohol that the brewers quickly withdrew their horses from the streets and headed for the barn.

Successful resistance can rout the enemy in every community where Christians will:

Prepare themselves with facts and faith
Develop a creative concern for persons
Render service without selfishness
Support good laws and honest officers
Make the church a vital force in the community

[1] Vance Packard, *The Hidden Persuaders* (New York: David McKay Co., Inc., 1957).
[2] Keeler and Efron, *Selected Statistical Tables on Alcoholism.*
[3] *Accident Facts* (1957 ed.; Chicago: National Safety Council), p. 51.
[4] *Ibid.* See also Roger Burgess, *Drinking Problems* (TEM Press), pp. 7-8.
[5] *Ibid.*, p. 5.
[6] John Wesley, "The Use of Money" (J. D. Booth, York), 4th ed., pp. 128-29.
[7] Harry Emerson Fosdick.
[8] "25 Years of Liquor Promotion," American Business Men's Foundation, 431 S. Dearborn Street, Chicago.
[9] Abraham Lincoln, "Address Before the Springfield Washingtonian Temperance Society," Springfield, Illinois, February 22, 1842.

IV

CAUTION FOR FAMILIES

"Train up a child in the way he should go, and when he is old he will not depart from it."
(Prov. 22:6.)

One of the major efforts of the allied alcohol interests during the past ten years has been to introduce intoxicants as a normal part of better family living. By identifying alcohol with home life, the trade would accomplish two objectives: acceptance and profits.

Since women have 80 per cent of America's purchasing power and the major portion of its prestige, why not put alcohol on gala display and make it a pickup "must" at every convenient shopping center? Then it might be easier for parents to be normal with their drinking.

But what about the children? They have a right to know the truth about alcohol. How much training, and what kind, will they get from modern homes?

Some parents feel that they should teach their children how to drink. It may be that what they want is to justify their own uses of alcohol. However, it is more likely that they want to train their children to handle

47

well what they consider inevitable social uses of alcoholic beverages.

Other parents take such a harsh attitude toward drinking that children never receive intelligent guidance on the subject. Since alcohol is strictly taboo with these parents, their adolescents never get calm answers to questions about drinking problems.

Parents can be inspired to take the time to discuss simple things about which children need to form convictions. The TV constantly attracts them with clever devices that often only deceive. The idea that everyone is drinking because "beer belongs" can be met head on by demonstrations of better things. Then parents will be able to show children just where beer actually does belong. When it is insisted that "where there's life, there's Bud," it will not be difficult to document the kind of life or death "Bud" really produces.

Of course, there is strength in a slogan. Nearly everyone is convinced that a brand of beer made Milwaukee famous, although brewing ranks about fifth in the leading industries of Wisconsin.

So much support was found for the claim that "vodka leaves you breathless," that the slogan has been dropped by advertising agencies. A few correctly stated statistics on death rates from drinking will often do the job.

To be sure, there are those who could get along to their own satisfaction without very much discussion of temperance. In one such case, the time had come at school to talk about alcohol. The amiable teacher, wanting the proper approach, said, "Boys, what should I talk about?" One said, "About two minutes and quit."

Some questions are more difficult at certain times. Bishop William C. Martin tells of the youngster who asked her church-school teacher, "Why do angels climb up ladders when they could use their wings to fly?" After a moment of reflection, the teacher replied, "Now that is a good question. Who has another?"

However, young people really want to know what attitudes their mothers, fathers, and teachers expect them to take toward drinking. We quite agree with a *Christian Century* editorial which insisted that neither parents nor churches have any right to keep silent. Anyone should know enough of the consequences of drinking to realize that everyone is somehow affected by it.

Observe the life of youth at any level, and you will soon discover that the pressure is on to drink. What answer can be given to the reasonable question, "Why shouldn't I drink?" If you are uncertain about the facts, find answers in the good literature now abundantly available. Be ready to support your opinions with scientific verifications.[1]

Some parents say, "Don't drink until you are twenty-one." Are those who use this procedure trying to rationalize their own drinking? It is usually interpreted by youth as meaning, "Alcohol is for mature persons—wait till you are grown." The liquor interests capitalize on it by using slogans which encourage drinking because "grown up now, you have come of age."

Mrs. Grace Overton was a guest in a home where drinks were served before dinner. Her polite "no, thank you" impressed the little daughter of the host who said, "Daddy, isn't Mrs. Overton old enough to drink either?" The father could only reply, "Perhaps our guest is old enough to know better." He wasn't prepared for this rejoinder: "Daddy, when are you going to be old enough to know better?"

What's the matter with the idea of teaching children how to hold their liquor, or enjoy themselves in social drinking? Would the practice be worth the risks? Are there no better uses of their capacity for leadership? Would this be the best way to teach them how to help others solve the complex alcohol problem?

Informed parents who have earned the esteem of their children can train them: to refuse alcohol without apology; to take the initiative in providing alternatives; and to win respect for convictions by positive witness.

One may say No gracefully. There's never any excuse for discourtesy. If waiters should come with wine, "let them see the corners of your mouth turned up and your glass turned down." Young people quickly learn to order soft drinks, without feeling either pride or censure.

It goes without saying that elders may teach children to abstain, but if they themselves use alcohol, they actually train their youth to drink. There is documentary evidence that young people who drink at home drink more away from home. Likewise, those coming from non-drinking homes are less likely to use alcoholic beverages when they are on their own.[2]

Families sometimes unwittingly provide an atmosphere that is conducive to dependency. This too often leads children to drink. Jesus said, "It is inevitable that there should be pitfalls, but alas for the man who is responsible for them! It would be better for that man to have a millstone hung round his neck and be thrown into the sea, than that he should trip up one of these little ones." (Luke 17:1, Phillips.)

The children of alcoholics need special attention. The normal expectancy of alcoholism among the offspring of alcoholics is between 20 and 30 per cent, as compared with an expectancy of 2+ per cent for the population at large. Children are psychologically susceptible to this condition because of the chaos and deprivation in their homes. Real help to the family of an alcoholic with children is a long step toward prevention of future alcoholism.

How can parents be reasonably sure that their offspring will choose and love the alcohol-free way of life?

First, they can teach and live the truth that will make them free. There are many effective ways of convincing children that intoxicants do not satisfy. With the aid of statements by doctors, youth are impressed by the facts that alcohol puts brains to sleep, releases inhibitions, sears conscience, and impairs reason, will, self-control, judgment, and skills.

Second, from experience comes the assurance that abstaining parents can maintain the happiest homes. It isn't enough to ban drinking. Parents have the positive responsibility of beaming their homelife toward the bright and gay togetherness that leaves no need for intoxicants.

Consider two examples. One three-year-old says, when beer ads appear, "We don't like it 'cause it's not good." Grandparents had tried to dispel false impressions made by the advertiser. The other tot says to his father, "Dad, let's get some of that good beer." The father says, "But we have something much better"; and he takes his son to the refrigerator for orange juice which he likes and learns how to share with others.

Third, the solid help of the church is another source of security. Why does the church recommend abstinence? Not because it wants to limit or restrict the activities of its members. The church helps parents hold up the ideal of sobriety because clear minds and pure hearts can more perfectly love God and sympathetically serve men.

Glenn D. Everett, Washington journalist, writes,

I wish our church families would be franker with youth. I wish they would tell any young man who is going into the military service or into a civilian career in law, art, business administration, advertising, salesmanship, or any other professional callings requiring social contacts, that he is going to face the problem of drinking. He should know that many of his associates will drink and that drinking will be expected of him—unless he makes up his mind that he is going to refuse flatly and unequivocally.

Nobody shuns you if you do refuse. You don't lose friends —and you definitely don't lose influence. I don't care what the drinker says to cover up for his own weaknesses; he has an innate respect for the man who doesn't drink and who won't compromise on the issue.

The man who won't yield on that issue is not likely to yield to temptation or pressure on other issues, and people know it.[3]

Which young people are more likely to use alcohol? Those who in their homes, have not been motivated and conditioned for better living. There may be vitamin deficiencies or feelings of inadequacies that make some more susceptible to drugs than others. But youth who have had pleasure, inspiration, example, and proper guidance in the home are able to resist temptation and realize maturity despite frequent outside exposure to drinking pressures.

The church enables parents and children to appreciate and create right relationships in the community. It invites allegiance to the Christ through whom all may move with joy toward completion. The church provides an unfailing power that can spark the enthusiasm of youth to glorious achievement. It inspires initiative in providing opportunities for youth to say Yes to wholesome things.

Recommending the "reign of God in every department of human life," Everett Tilson urges Christians to "exert every possible effort in the hope of humanizing conditions under which men wage the struggle for character." Should we fail to discourage the practice of social drinking in the home and community, "We help turn the potential citizens of Paradise Regained into the drunken bums of Skid Row, and some of society's most promising people into the strait-jacketed guests of neuro-psychiatric wards." [4]

The church presents a Christ who can become the source of victorious life for all who will receive Him.

> I know not how that Calvary's cross
> A world from sin could free;
> I only know its matchless love
> Has brought God's love to me.
> —HARRY WEBB FARRINGTON [5]

It is about him that youth want to know. Those fortunate enough to see him demonstrated in the life of the home will likely maintain lifelong loyalty to the Highest.

---

[1] *Family Packet on Alcohol* (TEM Press, 1958).

[2] Straus and Bacon, *Drinking in College* (New Haven: Yale University Press, 1953).

[3] Glenn D. Everett, "You Don't HAVE to Drink." Published in *Youth* magazine (United Church of Christ). Reprints available from the National Temperance League, 131 Independence Ave., S.E., Washington, D.C.

[4] Everett Tilson, *Should Christians Drink?* (Nashville: Abingdon Press, 1957), pp. 108-109.

[5] Copyright 1910 by Harry Webb Farrington. Used by permission of the Hymn Society of America.

V

WHAT DOES "TEMPERANCE" MEAN?

"The fruit of the Spirit is . . . temperance."
(Gal. 5:22, 23 K.J.V.)

In many clear pronouncements the Bible exalts temperance. Because it does not spell out the command, "Do not drink!" some have concluded that temperance implies the moderate use of alcohol. Differing interpretations of the meaning and varying customs of drinking have posed a problem for which there is no simple answer.

We are often asked, "How can our church teach temperance when your meaning for it is 'abstinence'?" Across the years men and denominations have had interesting discussions and bitter antagonisms over the use, abuse, and nonuse of intoxicants. We are comforted to find that 75 per cent of the people of the world get along very well without beverage alcohol. It is unfortunate that the rest of us quibble over terms more than we struggle for solutions.

There are many sincere people who make a separate case for temperance, as opposed to drunkenness and abstinence. Since to them drinking supplies some values, the problem is not alcohol as such, but alcoholism. This school of thought claims that moderation is the answer. For these, the dividing line between drinking that is permissable and that which is forbidden hinges on the amount of the intake. "Excess," they contend, "is the thing that may spoil the true benefits of alcoholic beverages."

Their easy solution for drinking problems would be the light use of alcohol, or consumption of beverages with less alcoholic content. Some who hold this view are influenced in part by the ancient idea that fermented wine was valuable in religious ceremonials and common diet. They point to Augustine who defended the use of wine as one of the "gifts of God to man." He is cited as a typically "temperate man."

Now, the New Testament classifies temperance as a fruit of the Spirit. This is in opposition to drunkenness, which is a work of the flesh that alienates the Spirit. Temperance is most favorably associated with life's best values. It ranks first among the virtues of love, joy, peace, longsuffering, gentleness, goodness, faith, and meekness. These are vigorous graces, the enjoyment and sharing of which would seem to require extraordinary self-control. Thus, there is the need of an inner mastery, a rational governor, for the commendable implementation of the other Christian graces.

Can one safely ingest elements of food and drink that would obviously attack the normal processes of physical, mental, and spiritual digestion? Some interpret temperance as meaning the kind of moderation that can do just that. Others insist that the true meaning of the word, as applied to alcoholic beverages, is total abstinence.

While there have been notable groups of abstainers from the days of Noah to the present time, total abstinence as an absolute rule for Christians first got its modern emphasis among the Quakers. There are today in all churches strong movements that encourage non-drinking. These religious societies have, in many nations, large followings which sponsor effective education for total abstinence.

Some churchmen, however, act as if anything is tolerable that is not expressly forbidden in the Bible. On that reasoning, drinking is condoned. By similar rationalization, slavery would be permissible. Setting the neighbor's house on fire would be allowed. Can it be expected that a book written two thousand years ago, and translated into many languages, would deal specifically with moral issues not then apparent?

For understandable reasons the Scriptures outline general principles of faith and conduct by which changing generations, under the guidance of the same Spirit, may know what is right in particular circumstances. A case in point is the refusal of Christ to settle a quarrel between a man and his brother over the family estate. Jesus said: "Take heed, and beware of all covetousness; for a man's life does not consist in the abundance of his possessions." (Luke 12:15.)

What does temperance really mean? In Greek ethics, temperance was one of the four cardinal achievements of personal character. It was named among the other distinctive virtues of prudence, fortitude, and justice. Citizens learned that even virtues, when carried to excess, may become vices. They discovered, as we must surely know, that it is right to be moderate in the use of milk and meat, rice and raspberries, coconuts and cake. These are things, good in themselves, which people may use to excess. Gluttony is, therefore, the forbidden sin. Temperance would in connection with such foods mean moderation.

Reflecting early Christian attitudes, Paul said: "Every man that striveth for the mastery is temperate in all things." (I Cor. 9:25 K.J.V.) This probably had no reference to modern social drinking. Paul urged the churches at Thessalonica to "abstain from every form of evil."

Again, in the classic category of fruits of the Spirit, the great apostle represents Christian graces as outgrowths of integration with the "body of Christ." Being branches of the Vine, Christians become blessings to mankind. They will therefore avoid taking into their lives things that could cause separation from the Spirit and Source of true life.

One may rightly conclude that temperance in biblical terminology has reference to maturation under control of the Spirit, rather than moderation in the use of spirits. For this reason Christians generally prefer to think of temperance as moderation in all things helpful and abstinence from all things harmful.

Recall that the products of the vine in biblical times were used largely as normal parts of the diet. There were no exact parallels to the social drinking of today. Comparisons between early attitudes toward wine and contemporary acceptance of beverage alcohol will help clarify our conclusions.

In the Middle East, dietary drinking involved the use of both new and old wine. One was the freshly squeezed juice of the grape, the other was fermented. Most people had learned scrupulous care in the use of wine. Drunkenness was regarded as a sin and a disgrace. Early Jews were strongly disciplined against gluttony. It is probable that this evil was found chiefly among aliens who had infiltrated the Jewish population. These, with renegades employed by the Roman government, were regarded as "sinners." Because Jesus was especially interested in these "lost ones," the Jews accused him of sinful fraternization.

But the dietary drinking of those days establishes no precedent for the social practices of today. Four factors have radically changed the whole picture. These are: The needs of a hungry world; the necessities of a mechanized age; scientific knowledge about alcohol; and the development of modern beverages.

Refrigeration, sterilization, synthetic chemistry, and world trade have taken away any important need that ever existed for alcoholic beverages. Everywhere in the world there are preparations of milk, tea, coffee and cocoa, citrus and other fruit juices, carbonated drinks, malts and many other appetizing, healthful, and thirst-quenching beverages which have no added hazard of addiction or intoxication. These refreshing products give added significance to the growing concepts of temperance as true self-control. There is nothing in their very nature, as in the case of intoxicants, to destroy the will or dethrone the reason. One could practice temperance in the use of them.

With the development of distillation, fortified drinks pose new problems for individuals and society. How could users of strong drink practice moderation? How could men justify the conversion of grains into alcoholic beverages of more than natural potency? Would the pressures of a growing liquor industry permit even the strong to remain moderate?

When in later centuries public drinking places began to entice laborers and draw husbands away from their families, new social problems quickly emerged. As men continued to trifle away their earnings and strength in drunken brawlings, their morals degenerated and shameful poverty developed.

Then came the great industrial revolution of the eighteenth century, when the evangelical churches launched crusades and preached vigorously to save society from threatened ruin. They pointed confidently to the Bible, Christian ethics, and human need as spiritual authority for complete rejection of alcohol in beverage form. Necessity forced them to encourage nondrinking as the wiser and more nearly Christian pattern for all. They were spurred to relentless warfare against the liquor traffic which now demanded status and recognition as a taxpaying industry with a mission for the emerging world.

Churchmen are now challenged, as never before, to decrease the availability of alcohol because drinking has become a major factor in alcoholism, mental illness, industrial inefficiency, traffic casualties, and accelerated crime. Even those great denominations whose doctrines were formulated in the early centuries are carefully re-evaluating their scriptural interpretations and ethical standards in the light of contemporary developments. The communions whose theological concepts have been influenced by radical changes in the past two hundred years strongly recommend—and some require—abstinence as the proper attitude for their members. All are engaged in sponsoring studies and promoting new educational programs which are designed to inspire sobriety.

They point out that science has corroborated the claim that ethyl alcohol is a principal factor in unnecessary injury to people, and that other chemicals are better and safer for use in medical treatment. Men now know that alcoholic beverages are inadequate as a food. They supply heat without storing up energy, calories without vitamins, depression of the bodily organs without tissue replacements.

Temperance is being re-evaluated, and Xenophon's ancient definition of "abstinence from all harmful things" is gaining new respect. It is gratifying to note that drinking people around the modern world are now expressing a decided preference for the true drinks of moderation. The per capita consumption in America for 1958-59 was: 35.2 gallons of milk, 28.7 gallons of coffee, and 11.8 gallons of soft drinks, as compared to 14.8 gallons of beer, 1.2 gallons of distilled spirits, and .9 gallons of wine.[3]

This change to easily obtainable resources for better living, in contrast with the mounting complications of inebriation, invites a growing regard for true temperance. Today's temperate person is one who, needing no artificial ingestion of alcoholic drinks, enjoys and inspires the kind of character controls that make for abundant life. Thinking clearly, he comes to understand, to accept, and to love others more objectively.

The temperate person subjects himself to positive spiritual controls. He refuses to let anything enter his life that might destroy its equilibrium or its appreciation of the higher values. Whatever threatens imbalance or indifference he faithfully avoids. He seeks constantly to add to his life those graces that offer gains for Christ and goals for his fellow men.

The temperate Christian will first of all think clearly. Who can draw a line on drinking and say, "beyond this is excess"? Inasmuch as there is no clear scientific definition of moderation in the use of intoxicants, the churchman should be slow to subject himself and others to the risks involved in consuming them.

The Christian will first think and then try. Forgetting himself in his concern for others, the sincere person's next step forward will be an effort to set a good example in every situation. He will try to live consistently so as to become a lift and not a letdown for his associates.

He will do more. The Christian will trust. His confidence will not be in the ability to "take it or leave it alone." His reliance will be on God. Having made love his aim, the Christian will attach himself to every good thing that offers nobler outlets for the energies of his neighbors.

True temperance, then, is balanced living that inspires one to think, to try, and to trust. In its highest sense temperance is spirit-controlled Christian idealism that seeks to transmit to others inspiration for continuing sobriety. Never forcing his way of life upon others, the temperate person will be zealous to join with others in protecting society against exploitation.

---

[1] *Contact*, August 15, 1959 issue, p. 13.
[2] Albion Roy King, *Basic Information on Alcohol* (Mt. Vernon, Iowa: Cornell College Press, 1953).

VI

WHY ABSTAIN FROM ALCOHOL?

"Take your share of suffering as a good soldier of Christ Jesus. No soldier in service gets entangled in civilian pursuits." (II Tim. 2:3-4.)

"Why shouldn't a free American drink if he wants to?" inquired the earnest young officer. Back from a tour of duty with the Air Force, he was adjusting to relationships in the community. He went on to ask, "Why can't we adopt a realistic attitude toward alcohol?"

Does the church have a convincing answer? Our friend has a right to know why some churches stand for abstinence. He is ready to face the alcohol problem. Can he get help from his church?

Some churchmen reason that "alcohol is here—men have always found ways of drinking it—under proper conditions it can be successfully controlled—alcoholism may be avoided by moderate uses of the beverage. . . ." But forty-five to fifty million mature Americans, regularly urged to try this or that brand, have decided that many leading medical authorities are right: it is smarter not to drink.

The threat of alcoholism is one reason why concerned

people never touch liquor, wine, or beer. There are evidences that some people can drink moderately for long periods of time without perceptibly hurtful consequences. Studies are being made in Jewish and Italian communities where drinking is said to leave no evidence of alcoholism. A widely-read book has been written on the subject.[1] One is impressed with the fact, however, that notes of uncertainty throughout these studies leave us without documentary evidence or substantial scientific data. Some noted psychiatrists and able representatives of Alcoholics Anonymous stoutly deny the claim that "there are no alcoholics" among these groups.

Harry Elmer Barnes, professor of history at Smith College, once said, "If Americans would learn how to drink as gentlemen they could enjoy themselves without indulging in frontier wildness." In answer to which the columnist, Heywood Broun, observed, "This is just like a professor, unrealistic and impractical. Why do men drink if not to get soused?" This is why occasional drinking may lead to overindulgence.

Drinkers may learn to confine their intake, let us say, to "a couple of beers." But there is a tendency to shorten the periods between these experiences. How else may they get hilariously "high" or comfortably "tight"? Yet the strong will of the drinker and the rigid taboos of his group might combine to keep him from getting "drunk." Dr. Albion Roy King, in *Basic Information on Alcohol*, suggests that the person who intends to "control" his drinking is usually "thinking in terms of what happens to the body at the moment of the alcohol's effect, and

[that] he is thinking individually, rather than about the long time implications of two-beer drinking in our society." [2]

Does this thinking ever take into account incurred risks? Every user of alcohol is susceptible to addiction, because alcohol is one of the analgesic drugs and men are habit-forming creatures. Each drinker is a potential alcoholic. None of those who have hit bottom ever intended to lose self-control, or involve others in their personal problems.

Alcohol poses problems for innocent nondrinkers as well as for those who drink it. The physiological and psychological effects of casual drinking are, for many, even more demoralizing than chronic drunkenness. Other authorities agree with Dr. Haven Emerson (for many years public health officer of New York City) that "the greatest threat to the personality of the people of this generation is that of allowing themselves to be drugged into relative inferiority."

This is a possibility because the ethyl alcohol found in all intoxicants is both a narcotic and an anesthetic. Since it depresses the conscious processes and thus retards physical reactions, this drug in beverage form adversely affects personality development. Not a stimulant, alcohol slows down normal operations of mind and so anesthetizes inhibitions that the bodies and wills of drinkers, now "without brakes," often get out of control. [3]

Does this strengthen or demoralize the social and economic safeguards for which one would otherwise assume responsibilities? The detrimental social effects of certain kinds of drinking are incalculable. Every pastor, doctor, and counselor could bear witness to the fact that all too many innocent people must suffer unnecessarily because of the drinking of others. Alcohol blankets the inhibitions. Perhaps our young officer would find it rewarding to interview the community social worker, or inquire into the reasons for Community Chest drives.

The economic factors in drinking involve wrong uses of natural resources for which drinkers must stand in judgment before a hungry humanity. Insurance rates have skyrocketed in recent years because of the increase in accidents from drinking and driving. Industry suffers the loss of millions of man-hours, and the public pays for increased inefficiency and defective workmanship resulting from alcoholism.

Our young officer's inquiry raises some other practical questions. Doesn't alcohol meet human needs for excitement, sociability, relaxation, and escape? It is considered by many the quickest way to social acceptance. Others find its use the "shortest way out of difficulties" which are not easy to face.[4]

Alcohol loosens tongues and breaks down cultural barriers. It is a "social lubricant" that makes for gay conviviality among, and ready acceptance of, fellow drinkers —so much so, in fact, that good standards are often forgotten in social exchanges that leave only the unpleasant aftermath. Drinkers sometimes find so much excitement that their exuberance becomes uncontrollable. It is for this reason that strict controls are set up for liquor

67

dispensaries, and bouncers are employed by night clubs.

Those who feature alcohol as the ideal relaxer fail to state that while intoxicants reduce bodily tension, they also induce loss of other important controls. The drinking man's influence with family and neighbors is often jeopardized in delicate situations where the fully-awake brain might have been more responsive to basic needs.

Granted that alcohol is a temporary palliative, with some accompanying benefits, cannot religion supply a better solution for these realistic needs? And if it can, would we not be wiser to explore the superior advantages of abstinence?

Many people do not drink because they have found that by abstaining they can experience a "life with a lilt," which cocktails can neither produce nor inspire. They have discovered that through abstinence they are better able to meet the several areas of personal need to which we have just referred. In moments of anxiety, for example, they have found almost instantaneous relaxation with such a brief prayer as

> Drop Thy still dews of quietness,
> Till all [my] strivings cease;
> Take from [my] soul the strain
> and stress;
> And let [my] ordered life confess
> The beauty of Thy peace.
> —JOHN G. WHITTIER

Some find, in religious fellowship, escape from boredom through true self-forgetfulness and timely consideration of others. The longing for sociability becomes a lever to respectability when minds are clear and hearts are clean. Many individuals form new habits of thought and service that aid self-control and social concern. Morally disciplined persons learn how either to face difficult situations or to avoid the thing that would only incapacitate them for handling real problems.

Have you ever seen success turn to failure through drinking? One of many notable cases was that of an exemplary young editor who moved to my town. He wished to marry a young girl of the community, but her father objected on the ground that the young man's father, though a district judge, was a heavy drinker. He feared the influence might carry over into the life of the son. However, the marriage took place—followed by complete family acceptance—and there was perfect happiness in the home of the newlyweds. The years passed, and a baby was born. Then, without warning, the beloved little one suddenly died.

The old judge urged his grief-stricken son to take a quart of "good whisky" for relief from his anguish. It was the young man's first drink, but it was the beginning of a living hell in the home of this lovely girl. The man's fine character, bright mind, and radiant personality changed for the worse, and his home life was utterly ruined. His ability for handling extraordinary problems was rendered ineffective by the deadening influence of alcohol upon his will.

Why shouldn't I drink on special occasions? Would this help you to develop a higher sense of social responsibility? Living among people involves more than enjoying oneself. It requires the giving of one's best. That is why we fight for our country, participate in community activities, and perform services beyond the call of duty. Real problems are faced more intelligently by people with sober minds. Helpful concern is best demonstrated by persons who employ their highest potentialities in the service of peacemaking. This requires a clear head and positive endeavor. Am I not in a stronger position to meet the crises of life without alcohol? The Bible helps us to appreciate that life can be more abundant without beverage alcohol. It does not spell out the formal command to refrain from all uses of liquor, but it leaves no doubt that abstainers have a better chance than others to achieve highest Christian goals.

One of the major efforts of our day is to remove from the drinking custom any suggestion of moral stigma. If the "sense of guilt" for drinking could be taken away, it is claimed, "people might learn to handle intoxicants reasonably well." If from Bible interpretation any real condemnation of social drinking could be obliterated "the case would be made."

The proof-text method of interpretation often leads into controversy and confusion. Christian ethics, based upon the unquestioned spirit of Bible teaching, rule out the social uses of intoxicants for many conscientious churchmen. There is an interesting revision of the one proof-text most often used by supporters of the moderation theory. Heretofore, much has been made of the word "excess" found in the King James' version of Eph.

70

5:18. But the Greek word *asotia* does not mean excess at all. The correct translation is "wastefulness," "profligacy," "debauchery." Authoritative lexicons support the Revised Standard Version, which reads "And do not get drunk with wine, for that is debauchery." [5]

Any degree of drunkenness that "blurs the moral twinges" would bring one into serious conflict with the two great commandments. Jesus said, "On these two commandments hang all the law and the prophets." (Matt. 22:40 K.J.V.) Included would be the injunction against "killing" which, in New Testament terminology, would relate as much to what a man might become as to the body in which he is housed.

Better than detached scriptures, or strained interpretations of singular texts, is the understanding of four basic principles of the life which the Bible, as a whole, depicts.

First, *the nature of man.* We have seen that he is a person made for companionship with God and creative work among men. Capable of divine worship and self-determination, he has the freedom of choice between good and evil, life and death. Does drinking help or harm him in the exercise of his freedom? Does it improve his self-respect; strengthen his witness, and help him to be more useful?

Second, *what is the purpose of God?* Life is a gift that is enriched by the presence and power of the Giver. What behavior patterns will encourage the best use of the trusts extended and honor the plan of the Creator for every person and his associates?

Third, *what is the ideal of service?* If men are merely to enjoy themselves, or achieve limited distinction, they will fall short of their aspirations. True satisfaction comes only in unselfish service. Supplying men with palliatives never helps them "possess their possessions."

Fourth, *why do we belong to the body of Christ?* So that we may grow in personal and collective usefulness. As a member of the Christian community, I am, with others in the group, so to live and serve that Christ's kingdom may come and God's will may be done in all the facets of life. As one under his command for the common good, do I have the right to weaken both my body and the morale of my companions by indulgence in unnecessary drugs?

We know from Jesus' life, his teachings, and his example that things physical affect the spirit and its relationship with God. When drinking depresses the bodily functions, blurs the mental acuity, dulls spiritual perception, blocks receptivity, and demoralizes team effort, do I have a right to indulge?

Drinking actually sets up a rival god. Idolatry results from the illusion that intoxicants provide a more adequate source of life than God supplies. Remember *The Story of Mrs. Murphy?* This book illustrates how a drinker may become so enslaved to alcohol that drinking will dominate his life. In an unhappy marriage, the bottle instead of the woman became this man's bride—Mrs. Murphy. In real life the glass too often takes the place of God. Drinking causes one to be possessed by the wrong god, to follow the wrong leads, and to miss the

72

chief ends of useful life. Men cannot resort to crutches without losing a sense of adequacy. We can have no other gods before Him.

The gospel calls us to moral discrimination. We are to accept the reign of Christ in preference to the rule of the crowd. Paul says,

Don't let the world around you squeeze you into its own mold, but let God remold your minds from within, so that you may prove in practice that the plan of God for you is good, meets all his demands and moves toward the goal of true maturity. (Rom. 12:2 Phillips.)

Becoming "a good soldier of Jesus Christ" is a serious matter, demanding preparedness for action. This involves development of strength, conservation of energy, and avoidance of subversive entanglements. It requires knowledge of strategy, absolute loyalty to the cause, and self-denial to the point of sacrifice. In contrast, alcohol depresses, demoralizes, and weakens one for right decisions.

Timothy was to be Paul's successor in life's greatest warfare. To endure hardships as a good soldier he would keep himself unentangled from "civilian pursuits." Did this mean that he would remain away from social activities, or could he be "in the world but not of it"? The extension of the kingdom would require rigid discipline for conquest at every front of temptation. This young leader was reminded never to lose his sense of urgency, in season or out of season.

73

"Be careful that your own life is pure," said Paul. And then, remembering that his lieutenant was a strict abstainer, he went on parenthetically to suggest that instead of the polluted water of the country where he would campaign, Timothy was to "drink wine in moderation." Why? "It will do your stomach good and help you to get over your frequent spells of illness." [7]

Was this a license for social drinking, or a bit of common sense advice to subordinate his antagonism for alcohol to a prudent dosage of wine, for the sake of his stomach and the success of the larger mission? One must find the answer in the light of the "extreme necessity" under which the wine was to be used, in the life and character of the self-effacing teacher, and in the spirit of the total message to Timothy.

Wine was the best-known remedy of that day for an upset stomach, but there are better prescriptions today. Putrid water is no longer a serious problem, for there are cheap chemicals now available that quickly purify water for safe drinking.

Will anyone question the sobriety of the apostle who had given up everything in his life for the sake of the Gospel, and who could say, "I look upon everything as loss compared with the overwhelming gain of knowing Christ Jesus my Lord" (Phil. 3:8 Phillips)?

This man was saying to his successor in a glorious warfare: Take time and trouble to keep yourself spiritually fit. "See that they [men] look up to you. . . . Give your whole attention, all your energies, to these things [study, preaching, teaching] so that your progress is plain for all to see. . . . Keep clear of such things [that would prevent a clear Christian witness]. . . . Keep your commission clean [as you fight the worth-while battle of the faith]." (I Tim. 4, 6 Phillips.)

There is no stronger advice to the young serviceman of this complex space age than to "Take the greatest care of the good things which were entrusted to you by the Holy Spirit who lives within us" (II Tim. 1:14 Phillips). "God's solid foundation still stands, however, with this double inscription: 'The Lord knows those who belong to him,' and, 'Let every true Christian have no dealings with evil.'" (II Tim. 2:19 Phillips.)

If he really wants America to be strong in bearing freedom's torch in a frustrated world, our soldier will re-evaluate the superior merits of sobriety.

[1] Charles R. Snyder, *Alcohol and the Jews* (New Haven: The Free Press and Yale School of Alcohol Studies, 1958).

[2] Albion Roy King, *Basic Information on Alcohol* (Mt. Vernon, Iowa: Cornell College Press, 1953), pp. 136-37.

[3] *Ibid.*, pp. 73-82.

[4] *Ibid.*, pp. 26-45.

[5] H. G. Liddell & Robert Scott, *A Greek-English Lexicon.* Ed. and rev. by Sir Henry Stuart Jones. (Oxford: The Clarendon Press, 1940). James H. Moulton & George Milligan, *The Vocabulary of the Greek Testament* (London: Hodder and Stoughton, 1914). Richard Chenevix Trench, *Synonyms of the New Testament.*

[6] Natalie Anderson Scott, *The Story of Mrs. Murphy* (New York: E. P. Dutton & Company, Inc., 1941).

[7] C. Aubrey Hearn, *Alcohol and Christian Influence* (Nashville: Convention Press, 1957).

VII

PRAYER AND DRINKING PROBLEMS

*"If ye abide in me, and my words abide in you,
ye shall ask what ye will, and it shall be done
unto you."* (John 15:7 K.J.V.)

Prayer changes things; it also changes people. We
know that "the effectual fervent prayer of a righteous
man availeth much." (Jas. 5:16 K.J.V.)

There are times when premature attempts at prayer
may block solutions to problems. The inept use of this
great instrument of power has prompted some counselors
to warn against using this approach with alcoholics. Common sense and knowledge of human dispositions should
dictate when and how prayer can be most effectively
employed.

Early one morning, a drunk man came into a down-
town church office for help. Distracting the attention of
an associate pastor from other duties, he awkwardly asked
for the price of a meal. Instead of a lift, he got a lecture.
Angered by this treatment, the infuriated man was leav-
ing the church when he met the incoming minister of
education. This understanding person offered the man
a breakfast. He was not surprised to find that the drinking stranger wanted something more. Moving casually

into the little chapel the two sat together in quiet meditation. In an atmosphere of tender loving care it was the destitute man who asked for prayer. Following the conversion experience, adventures in the growing skills of prayer and fellowship brought new meaning and purpose to this transformed life.

Starr Daily tells of a businessman who complained that his "partner was drinking too much, and was spending beyond his ability. He took money out of the business that did not belong to him." There was great anxiety. A serious breach was inevitable. The thought of confronting his partner with accusations of dishonesty only intensified his unhappiness. He finally decided to deal with the matter in prayer. Finding his own peace in communion with God, he discovered how to communicate with his partner. The partner finally came to him with a tearful admission of his guilt, thoroughly penitent, and ready for reconciliation. The two prayed for direction. By means of prayer the light came, and with it came resolution. The solution was found when the partner gave up drinking and returned the stolen money.[1]

We do not understand how God uses prayer for our guidance in constructively influencing the lives of others, but we know that he does. There are many experiences which verify this truth. In his *Autobiography of Prayer*, Albert Edward Day supplies answers for our dilemmas.[2] Honest effort can develop most intelligent uses of prayer for those who will employ its simple disciplines.

No stronger testimony on the efficacy of prayer has come in modern times than the witness of Bishop G.

Bromley Oxnam in his book *A Testament of Faith*.[3] His own successful resistance to malevolent forces constitutes a most revealing story of God's availability and eagerness to answer the prayers of the faithful. When America's best-known international diplomat was ailing, he called for the great churchman to visit him. The first request that greeted Bishop Oxnam was an earnest appeal from John Foster Dulles for personal prayer.

Prayer, of course, needs the support of intelligent courage. Too many of us offer petitions to God without purposeful willingness to discharge our duty in the particular case. A little girl had been taught to reverence God but had not learned how to relate her responsibilities to his presence and power. It was after supper that the mother said to her daughter, "Please bring the broom from the back porch." When the child hesitated to go into the dark, her mother said, "Have no fear, don't you know God is everywhere, and will be with you out there?" Peering cautiously into the dark, her tiny daughter said, "God, if you're there, please hand me that broom."

From the Master Teacher comes the admonition that men "ought always to pray and not to lose heart." One of his greatest assurances to the disciples was that "If you abide in me, and my words abide in you, you shall ask whatever you will, and it shall be done for you." Jesus openly assured Peter, "I have prayed for you that your faith may not fail; and when you have turned, strengthen your brethren." (It is interesting to note that a physician was inspired to preserve this record—Luke 22:32.)

Christ also said, "If two of you shall agree on earth as touching anything that they shall ask, it shall be done for them of my Father which is in Heaven." In the well-known prayer with which he taught his disciples, Jesus suggested that we petition the Father to "lead us not into temptation."

Members of the Christian community and those outside need the constant protection and upward pull of "the higher Power," whom we call Father. That all are frequently exposed to terrific pressures which are contrary to best spiritual interests, no one can doubt. Perhaps the most glamorous of contemporary temptations are the varied inducements to drink more and more. Only those who "set the Lord always before" them can be certain of inner resources for consistent resistance.

The most reliable means of liberation of inebriates is dependence upon persistent prayer. Here alone is the ultimate power for breaking the tyranny of intoxicants. Victims of strong drink often experience delusions that only God can cure. A group of psychiatric physicians are now saying that drugs can take away demons from drunkenness. This has not yet been successfully demonstrated. But if such chemicals should be developed, how can we break the psychological power with which alcohol too often dominates men?

Far better than tranquilizing pills is transforming prayer. It can bring to men the strength of God for overcoming any disorder with which we struggle. Chemicals only allay imaginary problems while doctors help patients find the cure. Antabuse may make drinkers dislike alcohol, but appeals to Christ can give a peace beyond all understanding.

The church today has made available wonderful programs of education, commitment, rehabilitation, and legislation that really provide some intelligent answers to alcohol. But without the aid of effectual communication through prayer, these devices fall short of meeting real needs.

How can this tremendous reservoir of power become available to the average person? We hear Christ answer, "Ask . . . seek . . . knock . . . and it shall be opened unto you." (Matt. 7:7 K.J.V.) When saints and sinners begin to call upon the Lord radical changes in current drinking patterns will soon be made. Even "If my people, which are called by name, shall humble themselves, and pray, and seek my face, and turn from their wicked ways; then will I hear from heaven, and will forgive their sin, and will heal their land." (II Chr. 7:14 K.J.V.)

It is difficult to understand how prayer can help solve drinking problems. But there are evidences that it does.

For one thing, prayer shifts our center of interest from the self to God. Some men only go through the form of prayer. Remember the two men whom Jesus said "went up into the temple to pray, the one a Pharisee and the other a publican? The Pharisee stood and prayed thus within himself, 'God, I thank thee, that I am not as other men'" (Luke 18:10-11 K.J.V.) Still self-centered, he merely told God how admirably capable of personal management he was. But "The publican . . . would not lift up so much as his eyes unto heaven, but smote upon

his breast, saying, 'God, be merciful to me, a sinner.' . . .
This man went down to his house justified rather than
the other." Why? Because, emptied of selfish design, he
invited God to come in and take over the control of his
life.

Then, prayer transfers our concern from self to society.
When the publican repented he went first to share his
new experience with members of his own household. The
Orientals have something of this idea in the proverb
that says,

> If there's righteousness in the heart
>   There's beauty in the character
> If there's beauty in the character
>   There's harmony in the home
> If there's harmony in the home
>   There's order in society
> If there's order in society
>   There's peace in the world.

Men who pray become spiritually responsive. Communion with the divine makes possible the expulsion
from one's personal life of those things which block
growth and cancel out influence. When the hungering
soul is fed with strengthening food, ideals of service ex-
pand into deeds of helpfulness. Responsibility then becomes one's response to God's ability.

Finally, the greatest power is available when the body
of Christians pray collectively. Oklahoma's famed coach,
Bud Wilkinson, says, "The team that prays together plays
together—prayer helps the player find the right place

for himself on the team and gives the team a unified spirit it can never attain in any other way."

This was the idea behind the statement of our Lord on that memorable night in the Upper Room: "If you abide in me, and my words abide in you," right things happen as a result of praying together.

Little groups of interested people, willing to pay the price, can effect desirable changes in every community. Modern miracles are resulting from corporate intercession. Many authoritative books and verifiable experiences sustain this truth. Read Madame Chiang Kai-shek's *The Sure Victory* for a vivid picture of transformations in whole segments of today's society. What is happening in faraway Formosa can be realized on a larger scale in America, if we become sufficiently concerned about people who are in trouble.

For whom should we pray? Primarily for ourselves, that our consciences may be quickened, and that proper concepts of stewardship might stir us out of complacency. Who is doing anything for the hidden alcoholics in our churches? Are those of any skid row ever made to feel wanted in services of worship? Something more than saying "I'll pray for you" must be done for the alcoholics of our cities and towns. Needing hospitalization, many of them would be helped by simple hospitality.

Ministries to alcoholics and their families can be made effective through prayer. How else can we develop understanding of their situation? How else can "saints" acquire the grace to accept such sinners? Churches ought to be centers of concern for those who now depend upon alcohol as their savior. It may be your prayers, or the petitions of the group, that will penetrate the stubborn resistance of alcoholics to necessary treatment of their illness.

It was the praying Abraham Lincoln who was interested in a "temperance revolution" that would "manumit slavery," depose "a tyrant," heal disease, and assuage sorrow.[4] In furtherance of such a movement we, too, can pray that "even the dram-maker and the dram-seller will have glided into other occupations so gradually . . . that they will stand ready to join all others in the universal song of gladness" for victory over alcohol. Let us become so concerned for the souls of distributors of alcoholic beverages that their lives may be used for helpful service.

At a time when alcohol-related crime is rapidly increasing, prayer can alert the country to action instead of apathy. An attitude of dependence upon God would point out ways in which legislation can be enacted to curb the aggressiveness of the alcohol industry.

So great is the need of congressional action against the serving of alcohol on commercial airplanes, that pilots and stewardesses would welcome concerted prayers for the safety and sobriety of the people for whom they are responsible. It will take mighty faith in and exercise of this highest prerogative of man to move some lawmakers to action for the protection of American families against alcohol advertising over public media.

When we pray until God changes us, circumstances around us will change for the better. There will be no painful waiting for others to solve problems for which

83

we ourselves can supply the answers. Commitment to God will enable communication with those about us. Trust in the Almighty will supply the thrust of life that can stem the tide of death all around us.

A skilled young architect came to Washington to participate in a significant meeting of twelve hundred churchmen. While there he was hurrying out one evening to the Communion service which would close the convocation. Accosted by a panhandler who wanted coffee, the layman was seemingly unimpressed with the pitiful plea of the man. Brushing him aside unceremoniously, the steward proceeded to the cathedral. All during the ceremonial, he kept seeing that man of the street—dirty, unshaven, and hungry. Going back toward his comfortable hotel he searched in vain for this unknown bum. He prayed and tried to sleep. Returning presently to the only open shop on that street, the architect spotted his man. He told him of his Friend. They talked long over their coffee and food. The man confessed an awful story which could almost have been matched by that of his father confessor. The men prayed. They discovered that "tremendous power is made available through a good man's earnest prayer" (Jas. 5:16 Phillips).

[1] Starr Daily, *Recovery* (St. Paul: McCalester Park, 1943).

[2] Albert Edward Day, *Autobiography of Prayer* (New York: Harper & Brothers, Publishers, 1952).

[3] G. Bromley Oxnam, *A Testament of Faith* (Boston: Little, Brown and Company, 1958).

[4] *Abraham Lincoln and Temperance* (Washington, D. C.: TEM Press).

84

VIII

HOW CAN WE WORK TOGETHER?

*"Is your heart true to my heart as mine is to
yours?" And Jehonadab answered, "It is." Jehu
said, "If it is, give me your hand."*
(II Kings 10:15.)

One of the difficulties confronting the temperance
movement is the problem of teamwork. Many sincere
people who believe ardently in abstinence are not eager
to be identified with some others who espouse "the
cause."

Differences in motivation and method have always
presented barriers to successful collaboration in social
issues. Already a minority group, advocates of temperance
are often labeled "professional prohibitionists" and "fanatics for reform." How can divergent groups work successfully together? There is no easy answer.

Knowing that earnestness is never a valid substitute for
efficiency, some churchmen will not support, nor even
countenance, certain types of temperance leaders. Of
course, there are those who would reject any person or
agency whose zeal for social change might call for extraordinary action.

Many Christians who would open their homes for passing friends will not join hands against pressing foes. To "avoid controversy," men sometimes aid the opposition by taking no stand at all. To what extent can the concerned collaborate effectively with those advocating other viewpoints and strategies? The answer may be determined by the spirit of togetherness described in Karle Wilson Baker's "Pronouns" where:

> The Lord said,
> "Say 'We' ";
> But I shook my head,
> Hid my hands tight behind my
>   back and said
> Stubbornly,
> "I."
>
> The Lord said,
> "Say 'We' ";
> But I looked upon them, grimy
>   and all awry.
> Myself in all those twisted shapes? Ah, no!
> Distastefully I turned my head away,
> Persisting,
> "They."
>
> The Lord said,
> "Say 'We' ";
> And I,
> At last
> Richer by a hoard
> Of years

> And tears,
> Looked into their eyes and found the
>   heavy word
> That bent my neck and bowed my
>   head:
> Like a shamed school-boy, then I
>   mumbled low,
> "We,
> Lord." [1]

Stubborn differences can be resolved when a strong defense becomes necessary for survival. Wherever men are challenged by a higher loyalty, lesser apprehensions will be overcome. A thrilling story from the Old Testament reveals how conflicting approaches may be turned into co-operative adventures.

King Jehu of Israel acted on the principle that the test of true living is to take counsel not of our timidity, but of our courage. One day he set out furiously for Samaria, and on his way met Jehonadab, leader of the Rechabites. Legalistic abstainers, the Rechabites worshiped Yahweh. They managed to keep themselves free from contamination by the Canaanites, and they solved the simple alcohol problem of their day by the rigid practice of abstinence. Remaining in Palestine, the spiritual home from which these nomads never moved, they maintained their ascetic security at the risk of becoming socially stagnant. Jehu, on the other hand, was out to discourage drunkenness and other abuses by reforming the cultural atmosphere, even to the extent of slaughtering the priests of Baal.

87

Far apart as they were in their approach to life, Jehu and Jehonadad now were joined in one major objective: to exalt God. Their ultimate purpose was justifiable, though the means of attaining it were inadequate and, in some respects, indefensible.

Today, our expanding world demands growing ideals, traditions to be changed in accordance with the revelation of God and responsiveness of men. The Rechabite ideal, based on the principle of voluntary acceptance, must be freshly interpreted to the national mind and applied to private living. But cloistered abstainers need the companionship and drive of disciplined statesmen if communities are to be stirred from their apathy. If faith itself is to become secure, education for sobriety must be fortified by the friendship of many zealous Jehus. For wherever there is agreement of heads and hearts, the joining of hands will release useful energy for the Lord and his needy people. Only by such understanding and commitment can the Jehus and Jehonadabs of our day hope to ride together in a chariot that will lead to certain victory.

There is a great need for understanding, acceptance, and co-operation among groups that sponsor temperance programs. This could be the price of survival against the subtle onslaughts of a common foe. It may mean advance toward a sober society. We must either work together for mutual defense or perish singly for want of strength. Collaboration is essential for the full protection of the communities and common purposes we represent.

We have previously alluded to the possibility of nondrinkers sometimes teaming with drinkers even to achieve certain reforms. Some who are antagonistic to prohibition might be willing to join in the intermediate approach. Take, for example, the matter of alcohol advertising. There are many who regard the welfare of their children above the right to take a drink. There are many possibilities for cooperation, short of compromise.

Among abstainers and prohibitionists there is too much division. Some enthusiasts accomplish so little that in self-defense they turn abusively on those who do seem to be getting somewhere. Others have become so pessimistic that they are critical of responsible organizations which couple continuing hope with creative effort.

These attitudes have caused many good church members to ape the cynics in indiscriminate criticisms of those who purport to represent temperance. Not realizing that they are aiding the enemy, thoughtless churchmen shrug their shoulders at the mention of some temperance organizations whose activities have ever drawn the fire of liquor opposition. Quite willing to sit on the side lines while others are fighting with the team, these scoffers show no particular enthusiasm for any movement promising freedom from alcohol.

It is granted that some temperance societies have not in recent years attracted the right leadership. But considering the slander they have endured and the vicious propaganda through which they have lived, there is a lingering suspicion that God is definitely on their side. It is true that some methods have not been praiseworthy or powerful, but how much effort have we made to improve them? We of the churches certainly owe it to our-selves, and to the public, to be constructively co-opera-tive with all who are trying to safeguard humanity from the effects of liquor.

Not since the days of Frances E. Willard has the W.C.T.U. offered a more constructive program than now. What society does a better job of producing good audio-visuals, or encouraging sound alcohol education in the public schools? Now that more leading women, espe-cially young mothers and youth, are beginning to parti-cipate, greater work is being accomplished everywhere. Thoughtful critics who observe the new look of W.C.T.U. can never truthfully say that it has the "frown of the frump." Let us be sure that in our attitudes we are not, as some are, inclined to judge and to moralize.

What about the temperance league and united dry organizations? They also invite honest reappraisal by every loyal citizen. Such agencies are needed in every community to express united interdenominational con-victions. These societies offer channels for constructive service and action on behalf of interchurch groups. Too often the financial support of the churches is withheld because of mistakes that have occasioned embarrassment, or because of unusual methods which discriminate people cannot always endorse. But the remedy lies in requiring a better job of education within dry groups and encourag-ing more systematic collaboration with the policy-making directors of the organization.

No secular group, however, can take the responsibility of in-church training. The church leadership can neither pass the buck to full-time temperance workers nor bypass the duty of conducting among its own members a thoroughgoing program of alcohol education. But co-operation through responsible agencies can accomplish good results, community-wide. One of the purposes of the new Interdenominational Committee on Alcohol Problems is to help the churches develop within themselves more effective training programs for better character-building processes and intercommunity services.

Probably the most significant recent development is the program of alcohol study and Christian action now sponsored by many denominations. Councils of churches are becoming positively concerned. Study guides are now in preparation, and a five-year program of scientific research has just been ordered by the National Council of Churches. Churches may anticipate creative benefits from this joint investigation of our nation's social enigma.

But with continuing research we need renewed commitment. No one can take the place of the pastor or lay leader in discussing temperance, or in taking the initiative in temperance action. There is no substitute for the personal responsibility of preachers and teachers to prevent the effects of alcohol on men and women, boys and girls. All are affected directly and inescapably by the use of intoxicants. All Christians and nonchurch people, whether we like it or not, are inextricably involved; for drinking is a moral as well as a social and legislative concern.

Through all these developments there have been harmful, and sometimes untrue, criticisms of scientific schools of alcohol study and research. Well-meaning, but poorly informed, persons have stirred up more opposition than support for unbiased efforts of established laboratories to give us basic facts. Let us be as wise to discover service opportunities from these findings as the unscrupulous are shrewd to employ them for their selfish purposes.

There is so much to be done for unchurched people that no energy should be lost through interdenominational quibbling. It is much easier to sit in the seat of the scornful than to stand up for the success of a great cause. But "the hottest places in hell are reserved for those who in time of peril tried to preserve their neutrality."

There are people who would be willing to help in drying up the nation if they could do it in their own peculiar way. But even their way may not work. At 2:00 A.M. a drunk attracted an officer's attention as he clung to the lamppost and laughed. Pointing to a lighted sign across the street the hilarious inebriate said, "Officer, it can't be done, it just can't be done." "What can't be done?" the officer asked. "Why, look at that sign and see for yourself." The officer looked. The sign read "Drink Canada Dry."

The cure for delusion is attachment to a righteous cause. If people would find something big enough to live for, they would be less bored by what they have to live with.

A doctor says, "I go to hell and back with the alcoholic more frequently than with any other type of patient." Millions of worth-while people can be saved from this plight, if we have the courage to make the fight! To help

92

them develop new life patterns and to save others from needless hurt are objectives which are bigger than our petty differences.

It should be quite obvious that the real solution for drinking problems demands the collective thoughts and services of all mature Christians. A strong corps of capable leaders can be brought together from many denominations and agencies to form a solid phalanx for constructive temperance advance. But the movement can succeed only as its members follow the guidance of the Spirit. This is the only way to really know who are our true allies, to what ends we should work together, and by what source of power we may expect to achieve social sobriety.

Commissions of Christian social relations, temperance committees, and socially concerned townsmen can be drawn together in cells and groups for prayer and planning. Once spiritual power is generated (Acts 1:8; 2:1; 4:31), many service projects will take on new significance. There will be a new zeal for knowledge which will necessitate the training and use of skilled resource leaders, the development of a common language, and better methods of communication. Inspired members of the group can be organized and dispatched for a variety of creative services that will bring new life to the community and new respect for our work.[2] We need a new kind of movement in which all feel like members of the crew, not part of the passenger list.[3]

Those who put God in the center are not likely to get lost in the trivia of the circumference. Wherever there are groups of like-minded citizens, there can be a joining of energies to achieve worthy Christian goals.

[1] Karle Wilson Baker, "Pronouns." From *Burning Bush*. (New Haven: Yale University Press.) Used by permission.

[2] *Who Is My Neighbor?* A Handbook for the Commission on Christian Social Relations in the Local Church. Service Department, 100 Maryland Avenue, N.E., Washington 2, D.C.

[3] Elton Trueblood, *The Yoke of Christ*. (New York: Harper & Brothers, Publishers, 1958.)

IX

HELP FOR THE HELPLESS

"See, I am making everything new . . . . It is I who will give the thirsty man the right to drink of the fountain of the Water of Life without cost." (Rev. 21:5, 6 Weymouth.)

Who are the really dependent people of America? In a land of plenty there are all too many who are pitifully impoverished. Among these are the millions of men and women whom we now call alcoholics. Is there adequate help for these helpless? Experts have no easy answer or magic solution for this multiple problem.

In the past, drunkards were looked upon only as lost sinners who could either be brought to the mourner's bench or be damned. Always cowering under a deep sense of guilt, these outcasts seldom found "the cure."

Drunkenness today is called a disease, largely because there are treatments to which greater numbers of those affected will submit. The illness theory has a foundation in facts on the basis of which real help can be supplied for many.

The problem of alcoholism has become one of the nation's major health concerns. Doctors, social scientists, ministers, and citizens generally are giving serious study to find the best methods of coping with this growing peril. Churches are assuming responsibilities for counseling, pastoral care, and hospitalization never before provided for such sufferers.

Alcoholics Anonymous, Alcoholics Victorious, and other agencies have grown up in nearly all American cities of any size. In thirty-nine states citizens have supported legislation to establish rehabilitation programs. This alone highlights drinking as one of the most critical social problems of our day.

Now alcohol is not the sole cause of this widespread "illness." It is an ever-present factor. There are many contributing causes, but no known cases of alcoholism without alcohol. The more important fact is that the malady is getting out of hand. It is significant that alcoholics increase at the rate of approximately 150,000 per year! For more than 70 per cent of these, comparatively nothing is being done.

Chronic drunkenness results from a combination of physical, pyschological, and sociological circumstances in which repeated drinking produces dependency. Therefore, alcoholism is both a sickness and a sin. The alcoholic is a disabled, separated, and guilt-stricken person who is sick all over—body, mind, and soul. He is past self-help, a discouraged and broken person who needs Christ and the ministry of the church.

Who is to blame? The drinker, of course. But others must share guilt as contributors to this plight. The legalized liquor business and those who licensed the trade will face the judgment of God for allowing this condition to exist. The pressure groups that encourage drinking, and the "good people" who merely live to themselves, are all guilty of tolerating this type of delinquency.

Addicts do not all come from the neglected areas of the community. Many of the people who have become most helpless once enjoyed the highest prestige. Most of them could still be financially independent. Beside me one day rode an industrialist who, not knowing my vocation, discussed what he considered his "most serious personal problem." His concern was for the "cure" of a most valued inventor whose persistent drinking at the country club lockers had completely incapacitated him. Could anyone suggest the remedy?

We discussed the sickness and steps that might lead to his friend's recovery. Citation of many other cases where treatment was effective suggested procedures this man seemed eager to try. He left the plane with ideas that could help his friend.

Without dealing with the responsibilities of the state, let us consider the role of the steward in the program of rehabilitation. Whether the liquor interests or taxpayers are "made to pay the bill," concerned Christians must pay a price both for the prevention of alcoholism and the redemption of the alcoholic. When churchmen condone the liquor traffic by granting it license to operate, the responsibility for resultant damage becomes an extra burden for the entire community. Whatever else we may eventually do to shift the tax load to drinkers,

Christians must presently assume the duty of caring for unwanted drunkards.

These sick need every treatment we can supply: "drying out," proper diet, proficient doctors, and skillful care. In their destitution alcoholics stand more in need of acceptance than abuse. Their own sense of guilt, in fact, should relieve the counselor of any need for censure. In place of chiding or coddling, there is a demand and a place for guidance. Good stewards of Christ will become shepherds for these who have drifted away.

The compulsive drinker has already built a fence around himself, shutting out more than has been closed in. Becoming all wrapped up in himself, he has actually made a very small package. Being acutely conscious of this, the alcoholic stands more in need of reconstruction than reprimand. Can he find a demonstration of sufficient concern to convince him that change is worth the effort?

Roy Cash had his awakening in jail. Having come to the end of the rope, he decided not to "hang on." "Alcohol has mastered me for the last time," he said. With the help of a pastor and believing friends, he made up his mind to cut loose and do something for others. He was already dried out from sobering up in jail. What he needed now was the nurture and companionship that would give him opportunity, moment by moment, to amend his ways.

After accepting the fact that he could change his ways, Roy depended upon the Christian faith for the power to throw off the alcohol habit and take on new interests.

But his condition still required personal courage and medical care. He was built up by vitamins and kept going by vision. With new aim and true guidance, Roy came into the church and went to work. He found a job in the community as a tree surgeon, but he also began to "operate" a small congregation in the low-income area of the city. It was really an interracial aggregation of the unwanted. In time this became a most vital social service in the community. Roy himself has become one of the most respected citizens of the state in which he lives.

Like others caught in sin, all inebriates can be inspired to strip off "the old self with its doings," and be clothed "with the new self, which is being remoulded into full knowledge so as to become like Him who created it." (Col. 3:9-10 Weymouth.) "So if anyone is in Christ, he is a new creature: the old state of things has passed away; a new has come." (II Cor. 5:17 Weymouth.)

For the helpless there is the promise of recovery. The Bible supplies full hope of survival. Unrepentant sinners will be fittingly punished, while the saved will enjoy uninterrupted blessedness in the new life which confession and surrender can bring. Everything holds together in perfect order by the Love that now "makes all things new." Christ is our strong reliance. His language is redemption, not ruin. Through his grace and charm, even fiends can be transformed into friends.

Catherine Marshall tells in her recent book what it means "to live again." [1] One may have been strong in the days of prosperity, only to falter in the time of adversity. Then the truly penitent can start all over again and succeed. Now it is possible in restoration to be great in public life, successful with the famous. But one's deepest life is lived in fellowship with God. There is no satisfaction anywhere else.

It was for man's realization of this ultimate privilege that Jesus on the cross had said, "I thirst." To enable everyone to achieve adequate and eternal satisfaction, he had earlier extended the great invitation, "If any man thirst, let him come unto me, and drink." (John 7:37 K.J.V.)

Dr. Lynn Harold Hough says:

Every appetite is an indication of a legitimate satisfaction and for these satisfactions the God who made the appetite has provided. They represent an ascending scale. Some appetites will perish with time and do not reach out into eternity; but in the deepest sense of all God has put the passion for eternity in man's heart and then has given to him a thirst which only eternity can satisfy. This thirst the one on the throne declares he will satisfy freely from the fountain of the water of life. The drink of the heights belongs to the man who is destined for the heights.[2]

In the Sermon on the Mount, Jesus promises blessedness to as many as "do hunger and thirst after righteousness, for they shall be satisfied." We are creatures with physical drives and spiritual desires. When appetites "of the flesh" dominate, there is loss of direction in life, and men drift. But when human drives are subordinated to God's plan, life's higher virtues are developed, and the larger satisfactions come as by-products.

Many significant people of every generation could bear witness with New Testament writers that victory always comes to those who "live and act in vital union with Christ." Sin, being no respecter of persons, separates men from God. When we think of weak humanity, some of us feel as did General Booth about the staggering wastrel. With a look of compassion, he said, "There, but for the grace of God, go I." But remembering that help is always available, we take courage.

> Down in the human heart, crushed by the
>   tempter,
> Feelings lie buried that grace can restore;
>   Touched by a loving heart,
> Wakened by kindness, chords that were
>   broken
>   Will vibrate once more! [3]

There are many people today who also are following wrong leads in a vain effort to find satisfaction. They need to be reminded that it comes only through surrender of self, rejection of evil, and commitment to Christ in the service of others.

Shortly after entering the ministry, the little Ford and I tried one Sunday afternoon to go from the busy city to an appointment in the country. "As the hart panteth after the water brooks," so was my soul athirst for God. The people in this sparsely settled rural section had been sorely neglected. Thankful for my own new vocation and thinking of the message I would bring, I got lost on the way. Going back to the nearest telephone

I soon obtained these simple directions: "Take the first turn to the right from where you are, and follow the power line to the top of the hill. We will see you there."

Though the trail now led through hill and dale, a big jog here and a dog-leg there, the "first turn to the right" and the unfailing presence of the towering power line finally brought preacher and people together. We found the life-giving flow that quenched our thirst. Long after that sermon's content was forgotten, the text still lingered to bless: "Ho, everyone that thirsteth, come ye to the waters, and he that hath no money; come ye, buy, and eat; yea, come buy wine and milk without money and without price." For we did "go out with joy, and (were) led forth with peace: the mountains and the hills (broke) before us into singing, and all the trees of the field (did) clap their hands." (Isa. 55 K.J.V.)

As we preach and hear, God is saying still, "So shall my word be that goeth forth out of my mouth: it shall not return into me void, but it shall accomplish that which I please, and it shall prosper in the thing whereto I sent it." (Isa. 55:11 K. J. V.)

Any man may make this new beginning with confidence, for Christ definitely assures that "him who cometh to me, I will in no wise cast out." In the words of Phillips Brooks:

> Tell Him about the heartache,
>   And tell Him the longings too,
> Tell Him the baffled purpose
>   When we scarce know what to do.

> Then, leaving all our weakness
>   With the One divinely strong,
> Forget that we bore the burden
>   And carry away the song.

How can we best supply help for the helpless? Here are some methods:

1. Understand the problem of alcoholism. According to Selden D. Bacon, Director, Yale School of Alcohol Studies, this study must embrace a knowledge of alcohol, drinking, and the physiology and psychology of the human being.[4] Howard J. Clinebell, Jr. suggests that the study of this problem involves an understanding of how men use alcohol to meet needs the church ought otherwise to supply.[5]

2. Train laymen who will share some of their time and interests with those who have an alcohol problem.

3. Create an atmosphere of love that will invite down-and-outers into the company of those who care for human souls, regardless of their shortcomings.

4. Provide the excellent tools with which any group may serve effectively in this area of need.

5. Use Alcoholics Anonymous as a valuable ally in this vital service.

The church can take the initiative in education and action that will bring whole communities into vigorous rehabilitation programs. Informed members can mobilize a strong Christian witness to inspire research; organize prayer cells to substitute for bar patronage; encourage early treatment before problem drinkers hit bottom; provide real help to families, especially children, of alcoholics.

Preventing the "soil of addiction" must begin at the grass roots. It is there that personality damage begins to make individuals vulnerable to alcohol and even desirous of its anesthetic effects.

People will support the kind of Christian program that offers positive solutions for the problems that lie behind drinking and drunkenness. Best solutions are made possible by the quality of concern that brings men to Christ.

The following incident occured one Sunday in an aristocratic Baltimore Church. A drunken straggler dropped into the foyer as regular members assembled for worship. The brotherly usher welcomed this unkempt stranger, took him to a front seat and sat down by him. After the sermon, he introduced the inebriate to the pastor and then took him to his own home for dinner. There was redemptive help for one who acknowledged his helplessness. God was honored by the changes that resulted. When asked about the incident, Dr. Robinson said, "God is like that. This is His plan—transformation of the drinking man."

[1] Catherine Marshall, *To Live Again* (New York: McGraw-Hill Book Company, Inc., 1957).

[2] Lynn Harold Hough in *The Interpreter's Bible* (Nashville: Abingdon Press, 1957), XII, 532. By permission of Abingdon Press.

[3] Fanny J. Crosby.

[4] *Quarterly Journal of Studies on Alcohol*, Yale Summer School of Alcohol Studies.

[5] Howard Clinebell, Jr., *Understanding and Counseling the Alcoholic* (Nashville: Abingdon Press, 1956).

X

WHAT CAN ONE MAN DO?

"In conclusion, my brothers, delight yourselves in the Lord! . . . I do not consider myself to have 'arrived.' . . . But I keep going on, grasping ever more firmly that purpose for which Christ grasped me. . . . And with hands outstretched to whatever lies ahead I go straight for the goal —my reward the honor of being called by God in Christ." (Phil. 3 Phillips.)

There are times when we all feel that grappling with the alcohol problem is a hopeless task. When in such a mood, one is tempted to quit trying. The question often arises, "What can one man do?" Answers are not always easy to find. But encouragement comes with each assurance that "I can do all things in him who strengthens me."

The apostle Paul, who didn't find his own task easy, put it this way: I do not have all the answers, I myself have not arrived, but I keep going on . . . toward a real purpose. Great men, understanding their limitations, concentrate on the important thing they can learn to do well, and then apply the energies necessary to attain that end.

Even

> Felix the Cat kept on walking still
> By a train at Dover, got his tail run
>   over;
> On the rail he left his tail
> It gave the folks a thrill!
>
> But for all that he did not care
> And waving his nothing in the air
> Felix kept on walking still.[1]

In all areas of social service, success depends first of all upon believing that great things can be accomplished by individuals who have the will to persist. One man's temperance preaching was so effective that England's consumption of alcohol dropped within fifty years to less than one-tenth of its normal rate. One hundred years after that crusader's death, someone asked a Cornish native why he couldn't get a drink in that town. He replied, "A man named Wesley once wrought here."

This was the story back of prohibition in America. Persons like Benjamin Rush, Frances E. Willard, and Senator Morris Sheppard devoted their lives to abstemious living and adventurous witnessing for sobriety. A succession of lesser luminaries constituted a "line of splendor" that within two generations changed society from a drinking to a predominantly drink-free culture.

106

What can one man do against the odds of today?

> You are public opinion,
> You hold the power in your hand;
> You can change the course of events,
> If you take a determined stand.
>
> You are public opinion,
> You may stand for the right;
> You have the power, yes, you alone,
> But you must stand up and fight.

It pays to keep trying. The reward is inner knowledge that God is being served. When this is our motive, the results are always beneficial to society. As a member of the minority you are in good company. Le Comte Du Nouy in *Human Destiny* says that less than one per cent of the people supply the wisdom, the inspiration, and the will to change culture patterns and social norms for the better living of any generation.

Realizing the importance of developing consecrated personalities, Jesus said to Peter, "I have prayed for thee, that thy faith fail not: and when thou are converted, strengthen thy brethren." (Luke 22:32 K.J.V.) After the Resurrection, the Master asked him three times, "Do you love Me?" Receiving a positive answer, he instructed the changing man to "feed my sheep," "tend my lambs," "follow Me." Jesus was preparing all the disciples for significant leadership. Each would have singular contribution to the building of the kingdom.

Every individual today can, like Peter and the early

disciples, grow in Christlike graces. Ultimate solutions lie in individual consecration and spiritually enriched personal experience. Too many of us are content to remain religiously immature. We settle too soon into petty childishness and fail to develop powerful childlikeness. Prone to take the easier and less controversial course, we fail to remember that we are accountable for conditions both as they are and as they ought to be.

Recall Jesus' illustration in Matt. 11:16-19. Apparently it made no difference to these people whether a leader was, like John, an ascetic, or was one who, like himself, mixed freely with the people wherever he found them. Jesus was throwing back upon them their own words, expressing disappointment that these critics would follow any but their own way of life.

For John came in the strictest austerity and people say, 'He's crazy!' Then the Son of Man came, enjoying life, and people say, 'Look, a drunkard and a glutton—the bosom friend of the tax collector and the sinner.' Ah, well, wisdom stands or falls by her own actions. (Matt. 11:16-19 Phillips)

"So what," Jesus seems to say. "You condemn the gloomy, stern, sincere John, and hold in contempt one of the same Spirit who nevertheless looks upon life as a wedding feast! You find fault with both types of leader and will not keep faith with either one." They had failed to see that Jesus was meeting and mixing with men wherever he found them, not to compromise with their practices, but to empower them for living at their best.

The time had come when men should accept and

follow the true Deliverer. Friends were to go back to tell the now skeptical John what they saw: the transformation of men's lives through trust in Christ, growth where love had banished lust, peace of mind and rest for the souls of all who in simple faith took his yoke upon themselves. They were to cease their childish prattling, rise above pious pretensions, and devote themselves to the "weightier matters" of the kingdom.

Is this not our great need today, to follow where Christ is leading and to help men experience the maximum good rather than indulge the minimum "allowances" of Christian living? If we are to influence others for Christ, we must ourselves be truly Christian. It is patent that we are incomplete until we find our adequacy in him. The power by which leaders can become truly influential is through this living Spirit, ever standing at the heart's door and ready to enter. Admitting him is the first big step toward Christian maturity.

Sin, on the other hand, is love of the creature more than the Creator. Wherever Christ becomes central in the life of the individual and the church, there is less affection for substitutes and more love for the things that sustain abundant life. Souls that are sensitized by his presence have real understanding of God's will for their conduct. Such persons can share the kind of creative "intoxication" that men really want more than depressive liquors.

Paul cautioned that love demands maturity for its full flow. Perhaps he would also say today, "Christians should exemplify grace in their growth." This attitude of graciousness rescues religion from sourness. Good communication with people is blocked when churchmen are critical, repulsive, intolerant. They "frustrate the grace of God."

Christians need more than the wisdom of serpents and the harmlessness of doves. There is a "gentleness" which J. B. Phillips calls "adaptability." This means that in relationships with the herd there is both the possibility of personal growth and the opportunity of sharing "upper" values.

In the second epistle of Peter we are told how to grow graciously. "And beside this, giving all diligence, add to your faith virtue; and to virtue knowledge; and to knowledge temperance; and to temperance patience; and to patience godliness; and to godliness brotherly kindness; and to brotherly kindness charity." (K.J.V.) Thus we are urged to move from sterility to strength, from mediocrity to maturity, remembering that living is loving, loving is giving, giving is growing, and growing is God.

Such Christians so "delight themselves in the Lord" that they draw others by the sheer magnetism of Christ's presence in their lives.

Every man can also set a good example in his life and work. Pressing "toward the mark" he can avoid the sin of pride by inspiring others to

> Turn your eyes upon Jesus
> Look full in His wonderful face
> That the things of earth may grow
> strangely dim,
> In the light of His glory and grace.[2]

"If we are going anywhere worth the effort," says Dr. Hocking, "it will be upon the two legs of work and worship." To have a world fit to live in, we must develop a work fit to live for. This, of course, must be sustained by a faith that is fit to live by, finding expression in a self and society fit to live with.

Jesus supplies the home and horizon for our best endeavors. As pioneer of our faith, He is both the end and means of purposeful living. He is man's true motive and dynamic for positive goodness, and the only one who supplies both the challenge and power for highest possible achievement. Representing the greatest cause the world has ever known, Jesus is the mightiest leader men have ever followed.

His program is love and his purpose redemption. Jesus makes the life of his followers equal to any task God wants done. Even now his Spirit comes upon, dwells among, and abides within as many as ask for him in simple faith. Closer than breathing and nearer than our hands and feet is this One, whom God has sent from heaven to be our earthly strengthener. It was this good news of which Paul was proud, because Christ was now to him "all, and in all."

From the heights of rapturous fellowship with Jesus, we must each come daily to the valley of human need. Here we find ample opportunity to help men face serious temptations victoriously. How can one person influence enough people to make any difference in the culture pattern? What can I do to stimulate intelligent search for real answers to current drinking problems?

111

Let us consider four realistic possibilities:

First, I can let the Christ in me make attractive "the more excellent way" for many. Wholesome enthusiasm for the better life, the cleaner neighborhood, and a sober society will become contagious. A Washington church-woman loved her community too much to allow a liquor store to move in without protest. She inspired in her church the organization of a commission on Christian social relations. This group joined her in establishing a citizenship committee. Properly informed, they now gladly testified at the hearings which followed, and the Board of Control denied the petition for a tavern in that section.

Second, I can so witness among my business associates that they will gain new respect for abstinence and even make new plans for nonalcoholic parties. This happened in an elite circle of Virginia people when one young housewife introduced a party with punch that contained no intoxicants. Others followed the example. All had a better time.

In North Carolina, a transformed church member was asked by his employer to go down to the liquor store and get the supplies for their Christmas party. He replied, "At my church last Sunday I signed a pledge that I would not use alcoholic beverages. Should I now help others to do a thing that I feel is wrong for me?" At that moment, a second employee approached and was told by the employer to procure the alcoholic beverages for the office party. He also asked to be excused, suggesting that he had found better ways to celebrate Christmas.

After considerable thought, the owner of the business called in his secretary. The letter he dictated stated that "we will have the office party at the same time and place as last year, but without alcohol."

One example is worth more than a hundred exhortations. Total abstainer Pat Boone says, "If my influence was responsible for leading even one boy or girl toward drinking, it would be too heavy a price to pay for any enjoyment I might get out of it."

Third, I can so pray and plan that others will help in providing wholesome alternatives for alcohol. Drinking will be deglamorized only when churches become vital centers of interest for people in our communities.

In an Oklahoma City church, the young adults and youth have for years made their church the center of such a delightful social fellowship that even their non-churched friends prefer this exciting association to any that offers alcohol as a lubricant.

In an Arkansas county, the youth were so inspired by prayer and purposeful living that their influence carried a local option election in sections where the "wets" had expected a three-to-one victory.

Fourth, I can make the Christian ideal so all-engaging that many will reject alcohol and seek new life in Christ.

One of my treasured recollections is that of a very impressive young businessman, who through the leadership of an understanding pastor was able to transfer his affections from a rival deity to the living God. I met this young father on the first Sunday of a revival meeting in his church. Despite the fact that people had to come to church in a heavy snowstorm, the three Sunday services had been most inspiring worship experiences. On Sunday night, when I much preferred to go to bed, this young man asked me to attend an after-service party.

In the palatial home to which we repaired, thirty-six young adults were gathered for a most extraordinary reception. After having delicious refreshments, we formed a huge circle and prayed. Following the prayer, the young man who was my lay host for the meeting, distributed "responsibility lists" of prospective new members whom some of the group agreed to win for Christ during the revival.

By the end of the week forty-two persons had been received into the church on profession of faith. I learned from the pastor that the dynamic leader of this young set had returned from World War II an almost hopeless alcoholic. Going to the pastor in desperation, he was led to Christ. Accepting the pastor's challenge, he reluctantly agreed to begin a new class for the church school consisting of people who were not attending any church at all. It became one of the great Bible classes of the city.

The young man enjoyed such rapid progress in his business career that he was offered the presidency of the city's leading service club. When he courteously declined, the board of directors discovered that his reason was a distaste for the custom of inaugurating new officials with a cocktail party. The club decided that they, too, could get along without this ceremonial, and followed the leadership of the transformed alcoholic into unprecedented achievements for their group.

As Christ lives and calls, each Christian may with confidence turn confession into campaign, decision into dedication, commitment into crusade, and enlightenment into enlistment.

[1] Joseph Fort Newton, *Live, Love and Learn* (New York: Harper & Brothers). Used by permission of the publishers.

[2] Alfred B. Smith, "Turn Your Eyes upon Jesus." Copyright 1922. Renewal 1950. Assigned to Singspiration, Inc. Used by permission.

XI

REACH FOR A VERDICT

"God resolved to save believers by the 'sheer folly' of the Christian message."
(I Cor. 1:21 Moffatt.)

Answers to the problems of alcohol have not been supplied by mere cautions against intoxicants. Nor have solutions been effected solely by what we have to say. But more people have been inspired to make right decisions about alcohol when the case for abstinence has been built on four positive supports: reverence for God, respect for life, regard for personality, and responsibility for an improved social order.

Never losing courage, optimistic crusaders for sobriety have remembered that,

> Though the cause of evil prosper,
> Yet 'tis truth alone is strong;
> Though her portion be the scaffold,
> And upon the throne be wrong,
> Yet that scaffold sways the future,
> And behind the dim unknown,
> Standeth God within the shadow,
> Keeping watch above His own.[1]

116

Whether speaking to the crowd, teaching the class, or counseling with individuals, purposeful leaders always reach for a verdict. They know that to inspire persons to make decisions for right courses of action is more rewarding than to pronounce anathemas against the "evils of strong drink."

Let us concede that there are more popular subjects with which to deal. It does not follow, however, that one who decides to present the facts about alcohol will be rejected. If motivated by concern and compassion, temperance proponents will get a hearing. Some of the most respected Christians of this generation are men who have "cried aloud and spared not" on the question of temperance. It is cowardice, not forthrightness that generates contempt.

Must one necessarily incur disrespect, even in the most scathing denunciations of drinking? Much depends upon the spirit of the opposition to "spirits." If in hardest warfare against uses the leader still reveals love for the users of intoxicants, he will hold their esteem. When young people see that elders are fighting for them, as they speak out against the things that hurt, they will reveal more loyalty to their church leaders than to community "leaners."

Some do not say much about temperance because of timidity. They may have less fear of official disfavor than of complicating the situation. Admittedly, ignorance of the program and dread of alienating alcoholics are factors that must be considered. But failure to hit the subject head on leaves the problems of drinking unsolved!

117

It were better, perhaps, that some denunciations of drinkers had not been uttered. Offering no solution, these statistical tirades only bury the baffled listeners in a sea of doubts and unresolved prejudices. The results are bewilderment, severance of communication, and loss of prestige. "If that's temperance," they say, "I'll go along with my drinking friends."

But there are effective ways of witnessing for abstinence. Many teachers are so well-informed and deeply concerned that they succeed in winning disciples as they make war on drinking. There is no valid reason why a true Christian cannot be both crusader and counselor! Many leaders are. Fully awake to facts and thoroughly alive to folks, they establish rapport and right relationships with people.

Let none of us forget the scriptural encouragement to Timothy, that "the spirit which God has given us is not a spirit of cowardice, but one of power and of love and of sound judgment." (II Tim. 1:7 Weymouth.) One may strengthen his appeal by admitting that he does not have all the answers, while creating confidence that he does know at least some of the solutions.

Reinforcement always comes through accedence with God's plan to help people. Knowledge of scientific findings plus acceptance of social responsibility will build confidence and supply resources for dynamic advocacy in this field.

> You say the little efforts that I make
> will do no good: they never will prevail

to tip the hovering scale
where Justice hangs in balance.

I don't think
I ever thought they would.
But I am prejudiced beyond debate
in favor of my right to choose which side
shall feel the stubborn ounces of my weight.[2]

Through the grace of God and the "foolishness of preaching," we can continue to be instrumental both in preventing alcoholism and in transforming lives of those who have been hurt by drinking. By the same method, consumption in America was so reduced during the first quarter of the twentieth century, that practically all Keeley Institutes went out of business for want of patients.

Have we looked so long at problems that we have overlooked the recent evidences of progress? While some are drinking so heavily as to increase the gravity of crime, alcoholism, and economic loss, the consumption of spirits is not now as high as the record of sales of the past decade.

Great encouragement comes from assurances that during the past few years there has been a 12½ per cent drop in the number of adult drinkers. This decline comes in the face of stepped-up advertising of intoxicants, plus rapid increase in total population. The decrease in "drinking population" is particularly noticeable in the young adult levels. There are reasons to believe that this lessening of interest in alcohol is also obvious among youth.[3]

The trend in America and many other nations is away from, and not toward, alcohol as a desirable ingredient of personal and social well-being. The tides of progress are with, and not against, the temperance movement. Studious observers now believe the people have discovered that the seller's greed for gold is greater than the drinker's thirst for grog.[4]

There is ultimate triumph for this cause!

> Workman of God, O lose not heart,
>
> .   .   .   .
>
> For right is right, since God is God,
> And right the day must win;
> To doubt would be disloyalty,
> To falter would be sin.[5]

Now if reaching for personal decisions is a part of the answer, how should we "preach the word, be urgent in season and out of season, convince, rebuke, and exhort, be unfailing in patience and in teaching"? (II Tim. 4:2.)

Treatments of temperance are more than assaults on alcohol. They should never be sounding boards for temper tantrums. Churchmen have no right to bury ideas and ideals beneath a mass of meaningless statistics. Nor will people be inspired for action by a lot of "dry" information.

One of the most exciting discourses of the Bible was Peter's sermon at Pentecost. Its theme was "Jesus, Lord and Master." The people who heard were "pricked in their heart," and asked, "What shall we do?"

All pleadings should become persuasive incentives. The reach for a verdict can move men out of valleys to victory. Both content of the message and spirit of the minister are elements in effectiveness.

Douglas Jackson says, "For effective 'temperance talks' prepare carefully the central theme, say it attractively in as few words as necessary, and shut up."

Don't allow yourself to be put on the defensive. Claims of the Licensed Beverage Industries can be answered pointedly and briefly. You don't have to answer everything. Be selective. Pick out the wiset way to prove just one thing the liquor advocate says is wrong. It only takes one fact to establish that he is unreliable.

However, if he can show that you are in error on any point, he has discredited the whole of what you say. Always be sure of your facts, and make the minimal statement with maximal certainty. Even the understatement on any phase of the contemporary drinking problem that can be documented will support your case.

It is more important to emphasize your reasons for abstinence than to magnify the sins of drunkenness. Furthermore, positive interest in the public welfare will get you farther than bitter excoriations of the pressure groups. Persons are always more engaging than problems.

Some claims of the opposition are ludicrous. Properly exposed, they will become laughing stock for discerning people. You can, by pleasing contrast, reveal the true advantages of sobriety over the ridiculous aspects of inebriety.

Having decided what ultimate results to expect, the minister or teacher will ask himself certain questions about particular content, such as "What type of sermon or lesson shall I prepare?"

The pattern will depend upon ordinary needs, extraordinary conditions, continuity of educational procedures, and the kind of community effort required for facing immediate problems. Some churches provide at least two major opportunities each year for special temperance presentations. These are World Temperance Sunday and Commitment Day. Citizenship responsibilities will suggest other demands for seasonal treatment of this subject.

The possibilities for good content may be strengthened by four typical approaches: Biblical, literary, biographical, and topical.

What the Bible says is of utmost importance to a full understanding of this subject. There are ways of treating these biblical resources which can be most helpful. Consider two of them: *textual* and *exegetical*. The Bible has many pointed denunciations of drunkenness. A good concordance will be most revealing. The direct references to the subject are sufficiently numerous and relevant that pastors and teachers should never be guilty of twisting any scriptures out of context.

It is always possible to make effective use of this "Sword of the Spirit" in "rightly dividing the word of truth." People will be more responsive if they are able to understand from Bible teaching who is speaking, to whom the words are directed, in what period of time the truth was revealed, how these principles reflect God's will for today, and what difference our acceptance would make.

Better than proof-texts we tend to use are principles of the Bible by which more accurate and effective approaches can be made. See for reference Eph. 5; Rom. 14; I Thess. 5; I Cor. 6, 10, 11, 14; II Cor. 3; Gal. 5; Phil. 3; Col. 2; II Tim. 1; II Pet. 1; Matt. 18; Mark 9; Luke 10; John 7, 15; and many other passages which more broadly bear upon fellowship with God and responsibility for society. People need to know the larger implications of these teachings in relation to contemporary life.

There are numerous resources also in up-to-date books that abound in facts for bracing up minds. Among them are:

Burgess, Roger. *Drinking Problems.* (TEM Press).

Tilson, Everett. *Should Christians Drink?* (Nashville: Abingdon Press, 1957).

King, Albion Roy. *Basic Information on Alcohol.* (Mt. Vernon, Iowa: Cornell College Press, 1953).

Bogen and Hisey. *What About Alcohol?* "Enemy of Christian Missions." (Los Angeles: Angelus Press, 1934).

Clinebell, Howard, Jr. *Understanding and Counseling the Alcoholic.* (Nashville: Abingdon Press, 1956).

Quarterly Journals of Yale University, Yale Summer School of Alcohol Studies.

Webb, Lance. *Conquering the Seven Deadly Sins.* (Nashville: Abingdon Press, 1955).

————. *Discovering Love.* (Nashville: Abingdon Press, 1959).

Wise use of good literature can strengthen the speaker's knowledge and power for convincing discourses.

Human interest stories never cease to impress listeners. Take, for example, biographies of men and women who have found solutions for their problems. In *Cup of Fury*, Upton Sinclair relates the life stories of many intimate friends who were overpowered by their appetites for alcohol. In your generation are many outstanding abstainers whose stimulating record of achievement can inspire hope that will dispel fear. These success experiences can be so presented as to become life patterns for many.

Then, there are topics dealing with contemporary needs which always invite great forensic endeavor. Look at some of the current challenges, such as:

"To Your Health" [6]

"Back the Attack" (against drinking and driving) [7]

"Safe Driving Demands Sober Drivers" [8]

"Slippery When Wet" [9]

"Life with a Lilt" [10]

"Jesus at a Party" [11]

How shall I select materials for temperance studies? Procure from a trusted church agency a catalogue of available and recommended resources. Evaluate these according to most authoritative findings of theologians, doctors, and social scientists. Pray for guidance in your personal preparation, that your conclusions may be divinely approved, scientifically sound, and simply stated.

Answers to the realistic inquiries of people can be simplified if their leaders will become more specific and sincere. We can improve our approach by using facts on which people may build faith, by being crafty without being crude, and by avoiding cheap jokes about the antics of "odd" drunks.

We can help persons find adequate solutions to many types of social problems if we maintain our enthusiasm. They do not like to come into our meetings optimistically and be sent away "misty optically."

Nothing so weakens the case for temperance as carking expressions of hate and fear. Discouragement is contagious, but despair is sin. There is hope for confused people. There are evidences that abstainers are far from alone. These ought not to be hidden from view by withering gloom.

If the spirit of Christ is in what we say, people will be moved by the message. All sermons should lead men to Jesus Christ. His spirit is the cutting edge we need for trimming the alcohol problem to size. Images of his presence in our lives can banish illusions of alcohol's power and dominion over men.

Positive preaching and dynamic witnessing will inspire the kind of decisions that make life worth living even in adverse circumstances. Remember that this short discourse must overcome in a few minutes the confusing arguments your people have been hearing all week. But careful tabulation of truth, convincing intonations of voice, and a calm sense of divine urgency can strengthen persons for withstanding alcohol and helping others to meet the pressures that drinking invites.

As a part of good temperance education one may profitably institute selective seminars. Youth and young adults will be glad to help in this supplementary ministry. There are always competent professional folk in the community who will give a good witness for abstinence. Use of panels and audio-visuals can helpfully illustrate a brief presentation of temperance. These may be followed by enjoyable discussion.

One of the most potent ways of lifting up temperance is to include relevant and timely paragraphs in many sermons and lessons throughout the year. This can be done without imbalance or neglect of other important social issues.

There are compensations for doing one's best through any sane method of approach. I remember preaching once on the rather crude subject of "Beer, Biscuits, and Boloney." It was in a brewing community where employees, business executives, and related interests had tried to believe and convince others that beer is non-intoxicating, that it is a good food, and that as "one of the good gifts," it supplies peculiar economic and social needs.

I did my best with the facts and presented them with a lot of force. It looked as if I had failed. Rushing away from the crowded church, I asked God to forgive. But within a few weeks public attitudes changed for the better, and social conditions improved. In a subsequent experience of worship, two young men were converted.

"It wasn't anything you said today," they reported, "but our change was made on the night you opened our eyes to see drinking as a problem rather than a privilege."

Honest advocacy of temperance can be life-changing when we care enough for people to make the appeal. This presents no easy answer, but offers the most positive solution for society's affliction with drinking problems.

[1] James Russell Lowell.

[2] Bonaro Overstreet, "Stubborn Ounces." From Hands Laid Upon the Wind (New York: W. W. Norton and Co., 1955). By permission.

[3] Roger Burgess, Drinking Problems (TEM Press), p. 2.

[4] Gallup Poll, 1958.

[5] Frederick William Faber.

[6] World Health Organization film.

[7] National Safety Council slogan.

[8] National Temperance League slogan.

[9] Highway sign.

[10] Lance Webb, Conquering the Seven Deadly Sins (Nashville: Abingdon Press, 1955).

[11] Lance Webb, "Jesus at a Party," North Broadway Sermon Series, Columbus, Ohio.